Cambridge Elements ≡

Elements in Language, Gender and Sexuality
edited by
Helen Sauntson
York St John University
Holly R. Cashman
University of New Hampshire

QUEERING LANGUAGE REVITALISATION

Navigating Identity and Inclusion among Queer Speakers of Minority Languages

John Walsh
University of Galway

Michael Hornsby
Adam Mickiewicz University

Eva J. Daussà
University of Amsterdam

Renée Pera-Ros
Goethe-Universität Frankfurt

Samuel Parker
University of the West of England, Bristol

Jonathan Morris
Cardiff University

Holly R. Cashman
University of New Hampshire

CAMBRIDGE
UNIVERSITY PRESS

Shaftesbury Road, Cambridge CB2 8EA, United Kingdom

One Liberty Plaza, 20th Floor, New York, NY 10006, USA

477 Williamstown Road, Port Melbourne, VIC 3207, Australia

314–321, 3rd Floor, Plot 3, Splendor Forum, Jasola District Centre,
New Delhi – 110025, India

103 Penang Road, #05–06/07, Visioncrest Commercial, Singapore 238467

Cambridge University Press is part of Cambridge University Press & Assessment,
a department of the University of Cambridge.

We share the University's mission to contribute to society through the pursuit of
education, learning and research at the highest international levels of excellence.

www.cambridge.org
Information on this title: www.cambridge.org/9781009591027

DOI: 10.1017/9781009591034

When citing this work, please include a reference to the DOI 10.1017/9781009591034

First published 2025

A catalogue record for this publication is available from the British Library

ISBN 978-1-009-59102-7 Hardback
ISBN 978-1-009-59099-0 Paperback
ISSN 2634-8772 (online)
ISSN 2634-8764 (print)

Queering Language Revitalisation

Navigating Identity and Inclusion among Queer Speakers of Minority Languages

Elements in Language, Gender and Sexuality

DOI: 10.1017/9781009591034

First published online: January 2025

John Walsh

University of Galway

Michael Hornsby

Adam Mickiewicz University

Eva J. Daussà

University of Amsterdam

Renée Pera-Ros

Goethe-Universität Frankfurt

Samuel Parker

University of the West of England, Bristol

Jonathan Morris

Cardiff University

Holly R. Cashman

University of New Hampshire

Author for correspondence: John Walsh, john.walsh@universityofgalway.ie

Abstract: This Element aims to deepen our understanding of how the fields of multilingualism, second language acquisition and minority language revitalisation have largely overlooked the question of queer sexual identities among speakers of the languages under study. Based on case studies of four languages experiencing differing degrees of minoritisation – Irish, Breton, Catalan and Welsh – it investigates how queer people navigate belonging within the binary of speakers/non-speakers of minoritised languages while also maintaining their queer identities. Furthermore, it analyses how minoritised languages are dealing linguistically with the growing need for 'gender-fair' or 'gender-neutral' language. The marginalisation of queer subjects in these strands of linguistics can be traced to the historical dominance of the Fishmanian model of 'Reversing Language Shift' (RLS), which assumed the importance of the deeply heteronormative model of 'intergenerational transmission' of language as fundamental to language revitalisation contexts.

Keywords: language revitalisation, queer linguistics, minority languages, language policy, gender-neutral language

ISBNs: 9781009591027 (HB), 9781009590990 (PB), 9781009591034 (OC)

ISSNs: 2634-8772 (online), 2634-8764 (print)

Contents

Introduction: Queering Minority Language Revitalisation

Michael Hornsby and John Walsh

The purpose of this Element is to analyse the role of queer speakers of minoritised languages in the ongoing efforts to stabilise those languages in contemporary society. The minoritised languages in question are indigenous varieties that continue to be spoken to varying degrees in settings ranging from Ireland to Catalonia to New Zealand, in contact with hegemonic languages such as English or Spanish. The language revitalisation paradigm that emerged in European peripheral sociolinguistics in recent decades focused on protecting and expanding communities of such minoritised languages, with priority often given to the reproduction of 'native speakers' based on intergenerational transmission within the heterosexual nuclear family. In parallel with the work of 'sociolinguists for language revival' (O'Rourke et al., 2015: 11), language policy measures in these areas frequently focused on supporting intrafamily transmission or on established school-based immersion programmes where children could acquire communicative competence. Joshua Fishman's seminal work *Reversing Language Shift* (1991), with its emphasis on intergenerational transmission to children in the family-neighbourhood-community nexus, essentially attempts to reconstruct communities of native speakers. It was highly influential in the 1990s in language revitalisation circles around the world, particularly in Western Europe. Scholars such as Romaine (2006) and McEwan-Fujita (2020) have since problematised the model, the latter pointing out that 'families are not homogenous sites of language transmission' (McEwan-Fujita, 2020: 294) and convincingly showing that (inter-generational) transmission involves 'not only parent-child and grandparent-grandchild relations, but also many other kinds of language socialisation relationships ... Adults can socialise other adults and can socialise children of all ages in many capacities (extended family member, family friend, teacher, coach, lunchroom supervisor, religious leader, store clerk, etc.)' (McEwan-Fujita, 2020: 296). From a queer perspective, we add to this critique in our contention that with its central focus on the patrilineal cis-heterosexual family, Fishman's RLS model excludes those practising non-normative sexual identities from language revitalisation and excludes queer people from community-based efforts to stabilise such languages.

In addition to the marginalisation of queer people within the revitalisation paradigm, both in terms of research and practice, the field of queer linguistics has largely ignored minoritised languages such as those featured in this Element and has been dominated by English or a presumption of English monolingualism, reflecting its academic origins in North America and the United Kingdom. Recent challenges to the anglophone lens include Borba's (2020) analysis of queer linguistics in Brazil (although not from a revitalisation perspective) and Cashman's (2018) work on queer Spanish/English bilingualism in Arizona. Reflecting the minoritised status of Spanish in the southern United States, Cashman analyses how queer people navigate unequal power dynamics between named languages, even if one of those varieties – in this case, Spanish – is hegemonic in other contexts. Work on minoritised languages with much weaker demographic bases is less frequent still but a subfield related to sociological/anthropological and linguistic aspects of the question is emerging. This includes more socially oriented studies by authors such as Walsh on Irish (2019), Hornsby on Breton (2019a), and Amarelo on Galician (2019), some of which emerged from a research network that developed within the field of critical sociolinguistics over the past decade on 'new speakers' (O'Rourke et al., 2015), people who adopt languages other than those acquired through primary socialisation. Although critical sociolinguistics has paid much attention to intersectional questions such as race (e.g. Grieser, 2021), gender (e.g. Heller, 2001; Pujolar, 2001; Koch, 2008), and migration (e.g. Márquez Reiter and Martín Rojo, 2019), there has been little attention to the social roles of queer speakers in language revitalisation or to questions of queering minoritised languages themselves in terms of gender-fair or non-binary morphology or in relation to terminology. Some recent exceptions in the case of Irish include *An Foclóir Aiteach* ('the queer dictionary'; Mac Eoghain, 2022) and research on LGBTQ+ terminology (Murphy and Mac Murchaidh, 2023).

The lack of attention in the literature given to queer speakers of minoritised languages, both within the revitalisation and the queer linguistics paradigms, reflects and highlights the erasure of LGBTQ+ people in minority language settings. Intersectionality, while it has the potential to expand on the 'experience of culture through identifying overlapping visible and invisible identifications with experiences of oppression and discrimination' (Cor and Chan, 2017: 117), this has not been systematically applied to minority language communities. As a recent study on intergenerational transmission by Kircher (2019: 14) notes, 'L1, proficiency, and attitudes on the solidarity dimension predicted a large proportion of the variance [in transmission] – but not all of it, indicating that other variables were at play'.

These 'other variables', including demographic variables such as sexual orientation and gender and other identity markers and life conditions such as family structure, socio-economic status and ethnic origin, are more than apparent when the transmission of minority languages is being discussed. We have already referred to the discursive exclusion of people of non-normative sexualities in Fishman's RLS model and this possibly reflects community-driven discourses on the survival of minority languages and the assumption that a family unit of two adults of the opposite sex and 2.4 children is the optimal scenario for successful language transmission. And yet there have been major social changes over the past forty years or so, which have seen greater recognition for the rights of women, non-white people, and LGBTQ+ people (and intersections thereof), in turn leading to an increased awareness of societal diversity, inclusive of minority language communities.

As the intergenerational transmission of many minority languages continues to break down, communities are resorting to other modes of transmission, out of necessity, to complement traditional mechanisms and secure language maintenance. Romaine (2006) points out that many language planners have ignored Fishman's advice to focus on the home and community, instead investing in the relatively resource-heavy strategy of teaching minority languages through schools to each new generation. A recent volume edited by Hornsby and McLeod (2022) takes up the challenge of greater representation among minority and heritage language communities, and shows how, for example, minority language transmission is affected by modernising trends which are universal and not specific to any one type of language community. In this Element, it is shown that families from a minority background in the Breton-speaking community (like families anywhere) can experience disruption and drastic changes in circumstances when parents/caregivers decide to separate. Furthermore, language transmission is not just the responsibility of the nuclear family unit but it can (and often needs to) include grandparents, the extended family and the local community in general, to ensure the next generation of minority language speakers.

Crucially, when considering how queer people can be involved in language revitalisation, other modes of transmission need to be taken into account as well. A number of chapters in Hornsby and McLeod (2022) look at routes of transmission for minority languages that are not necessarily intergenerationally based. For example, in the case of Upper Sorbian, transmission of the language through the agency of the schools needs to be accompanied by other factors (such as religious practice) if a new speaker of the language is to be accepted by the community (Dołowy-Rybińska, 2022). The successful maintenance of the highly endangered language of Guernésiais, it is claimed, lies in peer-to-peer transmission amongst adults, leading on to the development of proficient new speakers (Sallabank, 2022). However, what Hornsby and McLeod's volume lacks – despite the best efforts of the editors – is a case study of how queer people are involved in the reception and transmission of minoritised languages. It is the experience of all the authors in this Element that LGBTQ+ people *are* deeply involved in minoritised language maintenance and revitalisation, and yet, as we have seen, their presence is very much missing from the academic literature on the subject.

This Element, therefore, aims to fill that research gap by providing the first anthology of papers about queer language revitalisation in Western European contexts, with a response from North America. There are two main thematic axes: (a) the sociological/anthropological, focussing on the roles of queer people in language revitalisation and their participation in policy implementation and (b) the linguistic, focussing on how minoritised languages are adapting to the demands for non-binary or gender-neutral features, as is increasingly the case in hegemonic languages across the world. The first section by Jonathan Morris and Samuel Parker analyses the intersection of linguistic and sexual identities among speakers of Welsh by examining their perceptions of representation within the language community and participation in its promotion. Using a reflexive thematic analysis, Morris and Parker identify the coexistence of Welsh-speaking and LGBTQ+ identities as the core theme and sub-themes relating to traditional values, community, and the association of English with gay culture. Despite the heteronormativity of traditional rural Welsh-speaking areas, greater visibility of LGBTQ+ people is noted across Wales and awareness of LGBTQ+ terminology is on the increase. The authors argue that the ability to express oneself has a direct bearing on language revitalisation efforts, hence the importance of consolidating queer Welsh-speaking spaces in the future.

The second section relates to another Celtic language, Irish, which despite promotional efforts by an independent state over the last century remains in a minoritised position. John Walsh analyses the work of a queer arts collective, AerachAiteachGaelach, that creates spaces for Irish speaking artists to collaborate and perform. Noting that historical discourses of Irish national identity and language policy excluded queer people, particularly in the early decades following independence in 1922, Walsh argues that the work of AerachAiteachGaelach represents a breakthrough by allowing queer Irish speakers to play an active part in the revitalisation of the language on their own terms. He analyses a theatrical production by the group in 2021, a multimedia immersive experience telling the life story of one of the group's members, Alan Walpole, who emigrated due to homophobia but returned to Ireland and re-embraced the Irish language. Tracing Alan's changing relationship to Ireland and the Irish language over time, Walsh's article shows how language is interlinked with sexual identity and migration. It also underlines how the inclusive ethos of AerachAiteachGaelach allows Irish speakers of varying degrees of competence to reacquaint themselves with the language through the medium of radical artistic expression.

In the first of two sections with a more linguistic focus, Michael Hornsby examines the efforts to make a third Celtic language, Breton, more inclusive of LGBTQ+ people. With limited support from the French state and poor institutional provision in its own territory, Breton is strongly minoritised with a dramatic decline in the speaker base in recent decades. Leftist and feminist groups have nonetheless worked to make the language more gender fair, albeit along binary lines and often under the influence of approaches from French as the dominant language. Hornsby examines how more inclusive Breton terminology has been developed in the area of cultural production, for instance, in the reworking of lyrics of traditional songs. In a case study, he examines approaches to creating neologisms for a queer lexicon. While LGBTQ+-affirming language has been provided, often through voluntary effort, non-binary linguistic features are virtually non-existent. However, echoing the other sections, Hornsby points to the importance of greater inclusion of queer people as a way to enrich the base for future language revitalisation efforts.

In the final section, Eva J. Daussà and Renée Pera-Ros analyse the debate about gender-neutral language in Catalan, using social media data over a seven-month period. Although Catalan is a medium-sized language by international standards and has far more speakers than the other sections featured in this Element, it remains minoritised due to hostility from the Spanish state and a continued shift to Spanish. Emphasising the need for inclusive language to accommodate the expression of performative needs of speakers, the authors analyse tweets responding to proposals for gender-neutral language in Catalan. Focussing on a thematic analysis of tweets related to neomorphemes and neopronouns, they find that attitudes are mostly negative and may intersect with transphobia and other phobias. They also highlight the use of Catalan's perceived vulnerability as an excuse for linguistic conservatism and emphasise the potential cost to the language if the global trend of gender-neutral language is not adopted.

Long-standing and persistent attempts to minoritise speakers of Irish, Welsh, Breton, and Catalan have resulted in push-backs in the form of various revitalisation projects in each of the respective territories. Minority language speakers have been able, as a result, to find their own voice, in their own languages. Now it is the turn of queer minority language speakers to find their own voices in these sites of revitalisation and to resist the double minoritisation they have experienced over the years – minoritisation as speakers of non-majority languages, *and* their erasure as non-heteronormative speakers within their communities. The authors of this Element seek to open the dialogue with case studies from four particular minority language communities, in the hope that other communities will add to the dialogue in the future.

Intersecting Identities in Minority Language Contexts: LGBTQ+ Speakers of Welsh

Jonathan Morris and Samuel Parker

Introduction

In critical sociolinguistics, sociology, and social psychology, thematic and discursive approaches to data analysis have contributed to our understanding of the experiences of LGBTQ+ people and how they construct their identity (e.g. Katsiveli-Siachou, 2021; Surace et al., 2022; Santos, 2023 and chapters therein). Relatively little is known, however, about the intersection between cultural/ linguistic identities and other minority gender and sexual identities (Walsh, 2019). Specifically, the focus has been on how LGBTQ+ speakers express their identity through language rather than on the extent to which individuals combine a specific linguistic/cultural identity with their LGBTQ+ identity.

The significance of this intersection comes to the fore in the case of minority language bilingualism, where the minority language may be an important component of the speaker's identity formation along with the idea that the speaker belongs to a wider community of minority language speakers. Furthermore, minority languages are often the subject of overt language planning measures in order to ensure their survival. In this context, the extent to which speakers who identify as LGBTQ+ (as well other minority groups) feel able to express themselves fully and be accepted within the minority language community might have direct repercussions for the vitality of that community (cf. Hornsby and Vigers, 2018).

In this section, we aim to address the gap in the previous research by investigating the experiences of LGBTQ+ speakers of the Welsh language in Wales. Specifically, we aim to ascertain how LGBTQ+ speakers of Welsh view their Welsh-speaking and their LGBTQ+ identities, and the extent to which these identities are seen to intersect. We address the following research questions:

(1) To what extent do LGBTQ+ Welsh speakers perceive there to be an intersection between their LGBTQ+ and Welsh-speaking identities?
(2) To what extent do LGBTQ+ Welsh speakers perceive barriers to representation and participation in the wider Welsh-speaking community?

Firstly, we outline the research context. We then outline the methodology and proceed to the reflexive thematic analysis of the data. Finally, we discuss the results with reference to the context of minority language revitalisation.

Research Context and Background

The current work is not situated explicitly within an intersectionality framework to the extent that we do not examine power dynamics or discrimination faced by LGBTQ+ speakers of Welsh here (see Crenshaw, 1989). However, we ascribe to the viewpoint that an individual's self-ascribed identities intersect to varying degrees and that this intersection influences their lived experience (Burke and Stryker, 2016: 663). Secondly, an individual's lived experience is shaped, in part, by wider social power dynamics which are created by differences in intersectional identities (Angouri, 2021: 5). These power dynamics may lead to varying degrees of acceptance by the wider community on the one hand, or exclusion on the other hand, and have ramifications for the notions of both legitimacy and belonging. As Cashman (2020: 65) notes, 'LGBTQ people might present themselves differently, might bring different aspects of who they are into the interaction, and might do so for different purposes'.

The study contributes to our understanding of the experiences of LGBTQ+ speakers of a minority language, and thus presents an analysis of bilingualism through a queer lens (e.g. Cashman, 2020). The decision to focus on the lived experiences of individual Welsh speakers who identify as LGBTQ+ was taken because we make no a priori assumptions about Welsh speakers representing a cohesive social group. Rather, we aim to shed new light on the extent to which LGBTQ+ speakers feel part of the wider Welsh-speaking community (see Walsh, 2019 for Irish). The results of the study will therefore allow us to address how *greater* community cohesion might be achieved in the context of Welsh language revitalisation.

The Welsh Context

Largely due to the pressure of grassroots movements and, later, the creation of the National Assembly for Wales in 1999 (now called Senedd Cymru/Welsh Parliament), the twentieth century saw an increase in language rights for Welsh speakers, the national implementation of Welsh-medium and bilingual education for children from both Welsh-speaking and non-Welsh-speaking backgrounds, and more concerted efforts to revitalise the language through governmental policy (see, for example, Carlin and Mac Giolla Chríost, 2016, for a more detailed overview). At present, the current Welsh Government's aim is to increase the number of speakers to one million by 2050 and increase the percentage of speakers who use the language daily (Welsh Government, 2017).

It would be incorrect to state that civic and public discourse has ignored how more efforts might be made to increase inclusion for LGBTQ+ speakers of Welsh in Welsh-speaking public and cultural life. For example, efforts have been made to ensure that inclusive vocabulary exists in Welsh and is used in public-facing documents (Stonewall Cymru, 2016; Welsh Government, 2023). Within cultural events such as the National Eisteddfod of Wales (an annual Welsh language cultural festival, e.g. National Eisteddfod of Wales, 2022), LGBTQ+ spaces have been created and overtly LGBTQ+ themes have been showcased in various theatre and television productions (e.g. James, 2010).

While mention of LGBTQ+ speakers of Welsh is seemingly absent from official language policy documents, the Welsh Government launched an LGBTQ+ Action Plan for Wales in February 2023 which aims to 'make Wales the most LGBTQ+ friendly nation in Europe' (Welsh Government, 2023). This strategy makes reference to the need for further research on the experiences of LGBTQ+ people across Wales and, particularly, those in rural communities. In addition, it outlines a commitment on the part of the Welsh Government to provide Welsh-medium support services for LGBTQ+ people as well as encouraging the visibility of LGBTQ+ people in Welsh literature and education and meeting the needs of Welsh speakers in LGBTQ+ culture more generally (Welsh Government, 2023).

There continues to be calls from the LGBTQ+ community for inclusion and LGBTQ+ initiatives which are pertinent for the current study. In recent years, for example, questions have been raised around LGBTQ+ representation on the Welsh language music scene (BBC 2022a), the wider community's response to increased representation (BBC, 2022b) and the use of inclusive language in Welsh, particularly for non-binary people (BBC, 2023a). Furthermore, initiatives such as creating a LGBTQ+ local Eisteddfod continue to be under development (BBC, 2023b).

The study of LGBTQ+ identities in Welsh-speaking society is therefore timely and much needed. In a report commissioned by LGBTQ+ charity Stonewall Cymru and partner mental health charities, Maegusuku-Hewett et al. (2015) examined policy-making, service provision and social inclusion among lesbian, gay, and bisexual adults with mental health issues in Wales. They note that 'it is not known at the present time how Welsh and LGB identities may intersect and shape each other – the ways in which LGB individuals living in Wales identify and affiliate with [the] Welsh language' (Maegusuku-Hewett et al., 2015: 87).

Methods

(i) Data Collection and Participants

Full ethical approval for the study was granted by the first author's institution and all participants gave their fully informed consent to participate in the study before a date for interview was arranged. Participants were reminded of their right to withdraw from the study at any point and to ensure anonymity were assigned pseudonyms that are used in this section.

The data for this study were collected using in-depth semi-structured interviews with eight participants who self-identified as LGBTQ+ and as a Welsh speaker. They were recruited using adverts that were placed on the social media channels of the School of Welsh at Cardiff University.

Interviews took place online in Welsh, and were recorded, using the Zoom application. Interviews lasted for between forty and eighty minutes (average of fifty-five minutes) using an interview schedule that consisted of seven main questions with additional sub-questions that were designed based on the research questions. Participants were asked to reflect on their experiences of being LGBTQ+ and Welsh speakers before talking about whether they perceive a crossover between their LGBTQ+, Welsh-speaking, and any other identities.

The sample consists of eight participants who ranged in age from twenty-one to fifty-one. Demographic information about each participant can be found in Table 1. Five participants identified as a gay man, one identified as queer, one identified as non-binary and one as a bisexual woman. Participants had all grown up in different areas of Wales, predominantly in rural areas or smaller

Table 1 Participant demographic information

Pseudonym	Age	Linguistic background	LGBTQ+ identity	Region in which the participant was raised	Current location
Dylan	23	Family	Gay man	Southwest	Northwest
Mali	38	Family	Bisexual cisgender woman	Mid	Southeast
Rhian	21	Family	Queer	Northeast	Northeast
Tomos	27	English-medium ed.	Gay man	Southeast	Southeast
Ianto	23	Family	Gay man	Southeast	Southwest
Eirian	23	Welsh-medium ed.	Gay, he/they pronouns	Southeast	Southeast
Emyr	28	Family	Gay man	Southwest	Southeast
Morgan	51	Family	Gay man	Southwest	Southeast

towns, but at the time of interviews most were living in the larger towns and cities of Wales. In addition, several of the participants had spent time living in cities in England but had returned to live in Wales in recent years. Six participants had acquired Welsh via family language transmission, one participant had acquired the language through Welsh-medium education, and one participant had attended English-medium school where they had studied Welsh and gone on to complete a degree in the language. All participants were university educated.

We acknowledge potential limitations in the sample and aim to address them in future research. As stated previously, all participants were university educated and were either undertaking postgraduate studies or in graduate-level employment. Furthermore, and perhaps more pertinently, no participants identified as transgender in this research, which should be considered when interpreting the results.

(ii) Data Analysis

Each interview was fully transcribed by the first author and then also translated into English. The data was analysed using reflexive thematic analysis (Braun and Clarke, 2022), an approach that identifies themes and patterns across a qualitative dataset. Braun and Clarke (2023) refer to thematic analysis broadly as a family of methods and it should be recognised that there are a variety of approaches to thematic analysis across disciplines. They argue that distinctive features of reflexive thematic analysis are that researcher subjectivity is embraced as a resource for research and that the practice of thematic analysis is viewed as inherently subjective. Furthermore, they reject the notion that coding of the data can ever be accurate due to the inherently interpretative practice (Braun and Clarke, 2023).

Another important aspect of taking a reflexive thematic analysis approach is recognising the researchers' own positionality and relationship with the research topic (Braun and Clarke, 2023). The first author is a white, cisgender, gay man who was born in Wales and has learnt Welsh as a second language both through the education system and independently. He now works at the School of Welsh, Cardiff University, where he teaches linguistics to undergraduate and postgraduate students of the Welsh language. His background allowed him to undertake the interviews in Welsh and meant that he was fully aware of cultural references made by the participants. While this was arguably beneficial for developing a relationship with participants, his own position as a white, cisgender, male academic may have placed him in a position of privilege and created an unequal power dynamic in the interview sessions.

In order to counterbalance any potential bias on his part, the data were also independently analysed by the second author. The second author is also a white, cisgender, gay male academic who was born in England, currently resides in Wales, and is a learner of Welsh.

The transcripts were read by both authors and then coded separately by each author. Coding was conducted inductively, focussing on what the participant had said rather than attempting to impose pre-existing theory onto the data. Coding was reviewed and discussed by both authors and then organised into potential themes. During the discussions it became apparent that there was some overlap between themes and that several of the identified themes sat within an overarching theme of *the coexistence of Welsh-speaking and LGBTQ+ identities*. The three sub-themes are presented in the findings of this section with extracts from the interview data (translated into English by the authors) used to illustrate these themes.

Findings

The Coexistence of Welsh-Speaking and LGBTQ+ Identities

The thematic analysis identified that the key theme within the data was *the coexistence of Welsh-speaking and LGBTQ+ identities* which contained three sub-themes: *traditional values and rurality*; *English as the language of LGBTQ+*; and *representation, community and reclaiming spaces*. The theme structure is represented graphically in Figure 1.

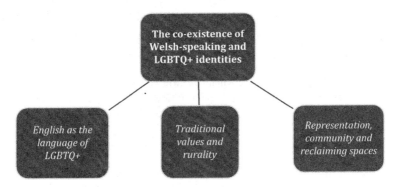

Figure 1 Thematic map.

(i) 'If I Wanted to Be Myself I Had to Be a Little Englishman': Traditional Values and Rurality

This first sub-theme focuses on the ways in which participants discussed the perceived heteronormativity of Wales and Welsh-speaking communities that they attributed to the dominance of traditional values and rurality. This theme was apparent throughout the interviews as participants discussed the intersection between their Welsh-speaking and LGBTQ+ identities. However, it was particularly evident in parts of the interview in which participants discussed their school and family experiences at a time when they first began to develop their LGBTQ+ identities. In the following quote, Dylan talks about his experience of coming out in a rural Welsh community and his relationship with an older family member.

> Ond o'n i jyst ddim yn disgwyl iddi hi fod mor *cutthroat* amdano fe, yrm, a bod yr agwedd yna, ti'n gwybod, y *reputation* a'r enw da a stwff . . . A fi'n credu bod hwnna'n *really thing* mewn cymunede fel [Enw Tref], yn enwedig cymunede Cymraeg gwledig.

> *But I just didn't expect her to be so cutthroat about it, erm, and that that attitude, you know, the reputation and the good name and stuff . . . And I believe that is really a thing in rural communities like [Town name], especially rural Welsh-speaking communities.* (Dylan)

Whilst later on in the interview Dylan describes having a good relationship with his relation, here he describes the challenges he faced when his sexuality was first discussed amongst his family. Dylan spoke about the importance of growing up in a close-knit rural Welsh-speaking community, and the reputation and 'good name' that his family had within that community. Indeed, it was him coming out as gay that he suggests not only threatened that reputation but also led to conflict with his older relation who most strongly held these traditional values.

The distinction between rural and urban areas was discussed by many participants, for example, Tomos, who talked about moving to a more rural area for university:

> Dwi'n meddwl, oedd 'na bryder ynghylch hwnna achos, wrth feddwl am bobl Cymrâg yn fwy cyffredinol, dych chi'n meddwl am bobl wledig, o'r cefn gwlad a pethe. Yrm, sydd, wel mae jyst y teimlad hwnna bo' nhw ddim mor dderbyniol â phobl yn y ddinas a pethe fel 'na. *So* ie, oedd ofn gen i am hwnna ond roedd fy mrhofiad i yn- oedd y rhan fwyaf o bobl yn dderbyniol iawn.

> *I think, there was apprehension about that because, when you think of Welsh-speaking people more generally, you think of rural people, from the country-side and things. Erm, which, well it's just that feeling that they are not so accepting as people in the city and things like that. So yes, I was afraid of that but my experience was – most people were very accepting.* (Tomos)

Tomos describes feeling 'apprehension' about how his LGBTQ+ identity would be accepted by 'rural people', suggesting that it was the rural location and community itself that was the source of this concern, rather than being related to the Welsh language specifically. Whilst he suggests that most people in rural locations were accepting of him, he uses specific contrasts with those 'in the city' to question whether this is always the case. Such contrasts were used commonly across the interviews, which may be reflective of the fact that the majority of participants had moved from rural to urban areas at some point. As such, many of the participants described the way in which they had only been able to fully develop their LGBTQ+ identity through moving away from traditional rural areas, particularly when they went to university.

In the following quote, Ianto describes his upbringing as being 'heteronormative', implying that Welsh-speaking life is equated to heterosexuality.

Dw i'n teimlo cynt pryd o'n i yn brifysgol, bod yn hoyw a bod yn Gymraeg yn eitha' *split*. Ti'n gwybod, doedd dim lot o *overlap* rhwng nhw. Yrm, ti'n gwybod, oherwydd bod bywyd Cymraeg yn fwy, *sort of*, teulu *heterosexual*, ffrindiau *heterosexual*, ysgol eithaf *heteronormative* hefyd.

I feel that before when I was at university, being gay and being Welsh-speaking was quite split. You know, there wasn't a lot of overlap between them. Erm, you know, because Welsh-speaking life was more sort of heterosexual family, heterosexual friends, quite a heteronormative school too. (Ianto)

The fact that Ianto refers directly to 'Welsh-speaking life' in this quote suggests that perceived heteronormativity led to a separation of his identities, leaving no space for his LGBTQ+ identity to develop at school or home. This is contrasted with his experiences at university where he suggests that his LGBTQ+ identity could take centre stage, implying that such spaces, and non-Welsh-speaking networks are less heteronormative.

When discussing the intersection of his identities, Emyr also considers heteronormativity and Welsh traditions:

I ryw raddau, ydyn, maen nhw'n plethu. Dw i'n credu. Yrm, dw i'n credu bo' 'da fi 'falle ddealltwriaeth o, neu hen synnwyr o, yrm, yr hunaniaethe Cymrâg a Chymreig a hoyw lle dyn nhw ddim yn dod yn agos at ei gilydd o gwbl a, ti'n gwybod, does dim pobl hoyw yng Nghymru. A mae pobl sy'n siarad Cymrâg sy'n mynd i'r capel ac yn priodi ac yn cael plant a *that's it*. A wedyn mae'r *sort of deviants*. A fi'n gwybod bod pobl dal yn meddwl fel 'na. Ond- a- mae hwnna'n effeithio arnot ti.

To some extent, yes, they intertwine. I think. Erm, I think that I perhaps have an understanding of, or an old sense of Welsh-speaking and Welsh and gay identities where they don't get close to each other at all and, you know, there are no gay people in Wales. And there are people who speak Welsh who go to the chapel and get married and have children and that's it. And then there are sort of deviants. And I know that there are still people who think like that. But – and – that affects you. (Emyr)

Here, Emyr offers a conditional acceptance of the intertwining of his LGBTQ+ and Welsh-speaking identities. He acknowledges that there is a perception of traditional values which rejects queerness and, in particular, he draws a contrast between people who 'go to the chapel and get married and have children' and what he refers to as 'deviants'. As he acknowledges, the heteronormative assumptions and traditional values which he associates with some Welsh-speaking communities have made it a challenge for his identities to intersect.

Drawing on the distinction between rural and urban areas already discussed, but also the distinction between linguistic identities of being a Welsh-English bilingual, Morgan offers a similarly stark construction of the intersection of his identities when talking of the 1980s.

Doedd 'na ddim profiadau hoyw drwy gyfrwng y Gymraeg. Doeddwn i byth yn darllen, byth yn dod ar draws, hyd yn oed ddechreuadau S4C, roedd yna ychydig iawn o sôn am bobl hoyw ar S4C yn yr wythdegau. Fyddech chi byth yn clywed unrhyw beth cadarnhaol ar Radio Cymru o ran bod yn hoyw na dim byd. Rhywbeth tu hwnt i Gymru oedd e. Rhywbeth Seisnig, rhywbeth oedd e ddim yn perthyn i ddiwylliant Cymru.

There weren't any gay experiences through the medium of Welsh. I never used to read, never came across, even at the start of S4C, there was little mention of gay people on [Welsh language television station] S4C *in the eighties. You would never hear anything positive on* [Welsh language radio station] Radio Cymru *about being gay or anything. It was something beyond Wales. Something English, something that didn't belong to Welsh culture.* (Morgan)

Reflecting on growing up in a Welsh-speaking community in this extract we see the intersection between representation and culture. Morgan's account suggests that these factors in many ways constrained his LGBTQ+ identity at that time. He emphasises this when talking about his first sexual relationship.

Oedd e'n beth rhyfedd achos, roedd yr elfen gudd 'ma 'de, mewn ffordd, yn rhywbeth Seisnig ond o'dd popeth arall amdana' i yn rhywbeth Cymreig. Ie, oedd e'n- y ddeuloiaeth yna yn, wel, naturiol mewn ffordd [. . .]. Os o'n i eisiau bod yn fi fy hun, yr adeg honno, oedd angen ifi fod yn Sais bach.

It was a strange thing because, this hidden element really, in a way, was something English but everything else about me was Welsh. Yeah, it was – that dichotomy was, well, natural in a way [. . .]. If I wanted to be myself, at that time, I had to be a little Englishman. (Morgan)

Overall, Morgan's thoughts on the eighties are clear: to be gay he had to act English. In the next sub-theme, we consider further the relationship between the Welsh and English languages and how these allow or constrain particular types of LGBTQ+ identities for speakers of Welsh.

(ii) 'Saying the Word "Hoyw" Sort of Feels Alien': English as the Language of LGBTQ+

In the previous sub-theme, we demonstrated that there was a perceived incompatibility between aspects of Welsh-speaking and LGBTQ+ identities that was attributed to rurality and the perceived heteronormativity and traditional values in rural Welsh-speaking communities. In the final example, we saw how Morgan had seen the need be a 'little Englishman' in order to assert his identity as a gay man. In this sub-theme we focus on the ways in which participants in this research constructed English as being the language of LGBTQ+ people in Wales.

The first quote, from Eirian, reflects how many of the participants spoke about their use of the Welsh language generally when speaking about their LGBTQ+ identity.

> Mae cwpl o ffrindiau fi sy'n siarad Cymraeg, maen nhw'n *like* naill yn *pansexual*, *bisexual*, neu jyst *like experimenting* a stwff *so* mae'n *really* neis siarad am bethau fel hwnna yn y Gymraeg. Ond, *I wouldn't say it's like* cant y cant yn Gymraeg achos bydden ni'n dechrau yn Gymraeg a newid i'r Saesneg achos mae'n fwy hawdd i drafod y pethau fel hwnna yn Saesneg achos rydyn ni wedi dysgu am y pethau 'na drwy gyfrwng y Saesneg.

> *There's a couple of my friends who speak Welsh, they're like either pansexual, bisexual or just like experimenting and stuff so it's really nice to like speak about things like that in the Welsh language. But I wouldn't say it was like a hundred per cent in Welsh because we would start in Welsh and change to English because it's easier to discuss things like that in English because we've learned about those things through the medium of English.* (Eirian)

Here, Eirian acknowledges that although they have Welsh-speaking LGBTQ+ friends, they might switch to English when having conversations with them about LGBTQ+ issues. Eirian appears disappointed that they are unable to have these conversations fully in the Welsh language and attributes this to LGBTQ+ issues being predominantly learnt through the medium of English. Other participants also suggested that this was due to not having LGBTQ+ specific vocabulary in Welsh, and a lack of use of particular words when they do exist, such as *hoyw* (gay).

> O hyd, dydy pobl ddim yn dweud 'hoyw', maen nhw'n dal yn defnyddio '*gay*', neu geiriau llai cadarnhaol wedwn i ond ychydig iawn iawn fydd yn

defnyddio'r term 'hoyw'. Ond maen nhw'n ymwybodol o'r gair, maen nhw'n gwybod beth yw ystyr y gair ond maen nhw dal yn peidio dewis y gair yn eu sgyrsiau bob dydd.

Still, people don't say 'hoyw', they still use 'gay' or less positive words I would say, but very few will use the term 'hoyw'. But they are aware of the word, they know what the word means but still don't choose to use it in their everyday conversations. (Morgan)

Morgan acknowledges that whilst there is Welsh vocabulary for words associated with the LGBTQ+ community, he does not feel that they are words that are used in everyday conversations. This could suggest that there is a lack of awareness amongst the Welsh-speaking LGBTQ+ community about specific vocabulary or that the English terms come more easily to mind.

The existence of this theme in the data raises the question about the degree to which LGBTQ+ and Welsh-speaking identities can fully intersect if speakers do not identify closely with Welsh terms. Ianto similarly describes a lack of identifying with the term *hoyw*:

Oeddwn i ddim yn teimlo bod y gair 'hoyw' yn ffitio fi ac oedd e'n swnio'n od yn fy ngheg i ddiffinio fy hun fel hoyw. Ond byswn i'n gwylio stwff fel teledu, caneuon, ti'n gwybod, y *cultural influences*, mae'r gair *gay* yn- fi'n teimlo'n lot mwy *socialised* o fewn e [. . .]. *So* mae dweud y gair 'hoyw' yn teimlo mor swreal 'falle, oedd e'n teimlo *sort of* yn *alien*.

I didn't think the word 'hoyw' fitted me and it sounded odd in my mouth to define myself as 'hoyw'. But I would watch stuff like television, songs, you know, the cultural influences, the word 'gay' is – I feel a lot more socialised within it [. . .]. So saying the word 'hoyw' felt so surreal perhaps, it perhaps felt sort of alien. (Ianto)

The suggestion of using particular words feeling 'alien' again brings into question the degree to which there can be considered an intersection of these two identities. However, whilst most participants described English as the language of LGBTQ+, Dylan suggested that this was beginning to change.

Nawr mae'r termau yn cael eu defnyddio lot mwy yn Gymrâg. A, ti'n gwybod, mae'r – mae e – *it's on that shift* fi'n teimlo a fi'n credu achos bod pobl yn gweld y shifft yna neu eisiau gweld shifft yn digwydd, maen nhw'n siarad amdano fe lot mwy ac mae pobl sydd eisiau dysgu hefyd eisiau dysgu a gwella eu hunan, *which is great.*

Now the terms are used a lot more in Welsh. And, you know, it's the –, it's – it's on that shift I feel and I believe that because people see that shift or want to see a shift happen, they talk about it a lot more and people who want to learn too want to learn and improve themselves, which is great. (Dylan)

Dylan equates the use of LGBTQ+ terms in Welsh with a more general 'shift' to discussions of LGBTQ+ matters. It appears that the existence and use of Welsh terms therefore facilitates wider conversations and allows LGBTQ+ speakers of Welsh to view their identities as more intersectional, despite the fact that all Welsh speakers also speak English and that code-switching from Welsh to English is a common feature of Welsh-English bilinguals' speech (e.g. Deuchar, Donnelly, and Piercy, 2016). This view was not shared by all participants, however, as exemplified by the quote from Mali's data following:

A does gennai ddim, ti'n gwybod, tystiolaeth empirig o hyn ond dw i ddim yn teimlo' 'mod i'n cael fy nerbyn, yrm, ie i mewn i'r gwerthoedd dinesig Cymreig yna fel person LGBTQ. Mae'n cael ei labelu fel rhywbeth *really* diweddar, *woke*, ffasiynol. Ond dyn ni wastad wedi bod yma.

And I haven't got, you know, empirical evidence of this but I don't feel that I'm accepted erm, yeah, into those Welsh civic values as an LGBTQ person. It's labeled as something really recent, woke, fashionable. But we've always been here. (Mali)

(iii) 'Is There Space at All?': Representation, Community, and Reclaiming Spaces

This sub-theme highlights how participants described LGBTQ+ representation in the wider Welsh-speaking community. Some participants, such as Rhian in the following quote, questioned the extent to which there was a space in Wales for Welsh-speaking LGBTQ+ communities.

Mae o'n bwysig ond dw i'n meddwl bod 'ne ddim gymaint o fel, yrm, sut dw i'n ddweud o, yrm, sdim gymaint o cyfle i fi gallu *sort of* mynegi fy hun yn y Gymraeg trwy'r ffaith fy mod i'n *queer, so* fel dw i isio ond mae 'ne ryw fath o *barrier* yn stopio fi. Chi'n gwybod, lle ydy cynrychioliad o pobl- neu *experience* fi, neu *experience* rhwyun arall yn y cymuned. Lle ydy o? Lle ydy o'n ffitio yn yr iaith Gymraeg? *Where's the space? Is there space at all?*

It's important but I think that there aren't as many, erm, how do I say it, erm, there aren't many chances for me to sort of express myself in the Welsh language through the fact that I'm queer, so I want to but there's some sort of barrier stopping me. You know, where is the representation of people – or my experience, or the experience of someone else in the community. Where is it? Where does it fit in the Welsh language? Where's the space? Is there space at all? (Rhian)

Rhian describes having a desire to be a part of a community of Welsh-speaking LGBTQ+ people but implies that these two communities exist separately and therefore the extent to which these two identities intertwine is more limited.

Later in the interview, Rhian offered a more positive outlook on changes within Welsh-speaking LGBTQ+ communities:

So OK dwi'n person Cymraeg sy'n siarad Cymraeg ac mae hynny'n un rhan ohono fi a wedyn LHDT mae hwnna'n *separate* ond dwi'n meddwl dros amser rŵan dwi'n teimlo fel dwi'n gallu dod â'r ddau beth at ei gilydd mwy, yrm, achos y ffaith bo fi'n cyfarfod mwy mwy o bobl a'r ffaith bo fi'n gwybod bo fi ddim ddim ar fy mhen fy hun.

So OK I'm a Welsh person who speaks Welsh and that's one part of me and then, LGBT, that's separate but I think over time now I feel like I can bring the two things together more, erm, because of the fact that I'm meeting more people and the fact that I know I'm not alone. (Rhian)

Whilst previously Rhian had suggested there was little space for her Welsh-speaking and LGBTQ+ identities to intersect, here she suggests that things are starting to change and to improve so that they are 'not alone'. Morgan also suggested that things are improving and that in part this is because Welsh-speaking LGBTQ+ people now have better representation in the media:

Mae'r rhaniad rhwng iaith a rhywioldeb yn llai nawr oherwydd y cyfryngau cymdeithasol, oherwydd dylanwad S4C mewn cymaint o wahanol ffyrdd a llai o ddylanwad y capel, eglwys ac ati [. . .]. Ry'n ni'n llawer mwy gweladwy oherwydd S4C, a cyfryngau eraill wrth gwrs. Mae'r newidiad hynny – efallai fod cymdeithas wedi dod yn llawer mwy goddefgar ond dw i'n meddwl ein bod ni'n llawer mwy gweladwy.

The divide in terms of language and sexuality is less now because of social media, because of the influence of S4C in so many different ways and less influence of the chapel and the church and so on [. . .]. We're a lot more visible because of S4C, and other media of course. That change – perhaps society has become a lot more tolerant but I think that we are a lot more visible. (Morgan)

Some participants also suggested that traditional Welsh cultural events, such as the National Eisteddfod, were places in which they felt free to express their LGBTQ+ identities. Such accounts suggest that the intersection of participants' LGBTQ+ and Welsh-speaking identities go beyond simply being able to speak about LGBTQ+ issues in Welsh, and that engagement in Welsh traditions also plays a key role here.

The Eisteddfod is the campest thing you can ever think of. Dyna sut dw i'n gweld e nawr, *like*, llefaru unigol *and how it's all expressive* a dyna be' dw i'n caru am y Steddfod mae fe – mae fe i gyd yn perfformio, mae fe i gyd i fod fel *expressive* a *over the top and camp* mewn ffordd a dyna sut dw i'n gweld e. A pob tro o'n i'n neud, *like*, cystadlu yn yr Eisteddfod [. . .], o'dd 'na fechgyn yn canu, o'dd ' na fechgyn yn perfformio, *it was like,* o, dyna be – *I've been like starved of.*

The Eisteddfod [cultural festival] is the campest thing you can ever think of. That's how I see it now, like, individual recitation [competitions held at the Eisteddfod] and how it's all expressive, and that's what I love about the Eisteddfod it's – it's all performing, it's all supposed to be like expressive and over the top and camp in a way and that's how I see it. And every time I was, like, competing in the Eisteddfod [. . .], boys were singing, boys were performing, it was like, oh, this is what I've been starved of. (Eirian)

The importance of both aspects of their identity was also noted specifically by Dylan:

Yrm, ie *so* fi ddim yn *really* teimlo bod 'da fi – bo fi'n fwy Cymrâg na beth i fi hoyw. A sai'n credu bo fi'n fwy, bo fi'n berson mwy hoyw na beth ydw i Cymrâg. Mae cael y dau peth yna yn *intertwine* – o efo'i gilydd yn *really kind of* diffinio fi fel person [. . .]. Hwn ydw i, *I am a Welsh homosexual.*

Erm, yeah so I don't really feel that I have – that I'm more Welsh-speaking than what I am gay. And I don't think that I'm a gayer person than Welsh-speaking. Having those two things intertwine together really kind of defines me as a person [. . .]. This is who I am, I am a Welsh homosexual. (Dylan)

Discussion and Conclusions

Minority languages are often linked to traditional values (e.g. Walsh, 2019 for Irish). At first glance, it could be argued that a barrier to a greater sense of cohesion between Welsh-speaking and LGBTQ+ identities is the perception that traditional Welsh-language cultural values normalise a heteronormative life experience which can often be seen as oppressive by LGBTQ+ people. The perception that minority language communities can be exclusionary has been found in other work in sociolinguistics, particularly those in the 'new speaker' paradigm (e.g. Hornsby & Vigers, 2018 for Welsh). We would argue, however, that in this instance the situation is more nuanced and that it is the perceived association between a Welsh-speaking heartland and rurality which merits further attention.

The deep-rooted association of tradition and rurality with heteronormativity can lead to a situation whereby Welsh-speaking communities, which are also often perceived as rural, can be seen as non-inclusive spaces. In the data, the perceived heteronormativity of Welsh-language culture and communities is often discussed with reference to rural areas. Jones (2019: 26) notes that 'it is an association between a [rural heartland] region and identity that structures academic, political and popular discussions about the nature and place of

"Welshness" to this day'. The perceived rurality of this region makes it difficult to disentangle perceptions of traditional values being associated with either Welsh-language culture or rural areas, the latter of which are often perceived to be more heteronormative than urban areas in work on gender and sexual identities in other contexts (even if this claim is increasingly questioned, see Driscoll-Evans, 2020: 12).

The dominance of English as the language of LGBTQ+ culture was also seen as a barrier to a greater intersection between Welsh-speaking and LGBTQ+ identities. While all participants were aware of the Welsh terms for these identities, most did not use them and felt that the equivalent English terms were either quicker to come to mind or felt closer to them (see also Schmitz (2021) on lexical choice in the Deaf-queer community in Germany). On the one hand, there were clear practical reasons for this considering that Welsh terms were codified and propagated later than their English equivalents. On the other hand, this sub-theme speaks to the wider issue of the association of English (and, more specifically, American English) with LGBTQ+ culture and has been found in other language contexts (see Boellstorff & Leap, 2004, and chapters therein).

Rather than represent a barrier to communication, we argue that the perceived lack in the circulation and wider use of Welsh terms for LGBTQ+ identities was symptomatic of a feeling that LGBTQ+ speakers have not been adequately represented in Welsh-speaking culture, and that it is this lack of representation which impedes increased cohesion between these aspects of identity. This was borne out more clearly in the data for the third sub-theme, where some participants questioned where the 'space' was for LGBTQ+ people within the Welsh-speaking community.

It would not be accurate to focus solely on barriers, however, and it was clear that experiences can change. A common thread across the three sub-themes was a perception that LGBTQ+ speakers of Welsh are more visible than in the past, and that this was a positive development which reduces feelings of being 'alone'. The benefit of greater representation can be explained by the principle of psychological coherence (based on identity process theory), which posits that identity can be weakened when an individual cannot perceive relationships between aspects of their identity structure (Jaspal & Bayley, 2020: 208). We would therefore argue that greater psychological coherence, facilitated by representation and inclusion, fosters a greater sense of belonging for LGBTQ+ speakers of Welsh. This is a valuable aim in itself but also increases the vibrancy of Welsh-language communities and culture in the context of language revitalisation.

Queering Language Revitalisation: How a Queer Arts Collective Navigates Identity, Migration, and the Irish Language

John Walsh

Introduction

One aspect of discourse around many of the languages featured in this Element is that they are purportedly unsuited to the modern, urbanised world and spoken by declining conservative, rural populations. In the case of the Irish language, such a perception is amplified by historical ideologies framing native Irish as a cornerstone of national identity, linked to a powerful Catholic Church wielding significant influence over public policy. This repressive ideological framework had negative repercussions for women, LGBTQ+ people, and other minorities, many of whom emigrated in droves to escape the stultifying cultural atmosphere. Although Irish language literature contains many examples of cultural and sexual transgression, since the foundation of the state a century ago Irish speakers have been useful scapegoats for failed cultural and social policy, and the perceived link between the language and conservativism persisted until recent times. The centrality of Irish to national identity has been challenged since the 1960s and the language is increasingly seen as a minority rather than a national concern. This shift has witnessed the emergence of cultural and social groups asserting the inherent capacity of Irish to give a voice to queer people. One such group is AerachAiteachGaelach ('gay, queer, Irish-speaking'), a queer Irish-language arts collective established in Dublin in 2020 comprising over sixty writers, musicians, dramatists, photographers, drag performers, and sound and visual artists. Many members of AerachAiteachGaelach are 'new speakers', people who were not raised with Irish but who have become fluent and regular speakers of it, often in parallel with their coming-out trajectories. This paper focuses on a public audio installation curated by the group, based on the story of one of its members, a gay man who emigrated to London in the 1980s but who since returned to Ireland, adapted to its changed culture, and became a new speaker of Irish.

Sociolinguistic and Policy Context

Irish is simultaneously a national, official and minoritised language spoken for the most part in Ireland but with speakers and learners in and beyond the Irish diaspora internationally. Although constitutionally the national and first official language of the Republic of Ireland and a core subject in primary and secondary education, it is spoken regularly by only about four per cent of the population although a significant minority claims good to very good competence in it. In Northern Ireland, Irish was oppressed for decades under unionist government and remains minoritised, but it gained recognition as an official language under the hard-fought Identity and Language (Northern Ireland) Act 2022. Irish is spoken mostly among the nationalist community in Northern Ireland, but efforts continue to spread awareness and knowledge of it among unionists.[1]

The 2022 census returns for the Republic of Ireland record 1,873,997 people or 40.4 per cent of the population as being capable of speaking Irish, a 6 per cent increase on 2016. The counties with the highest percentages of speakers are Galway (50%) and Clare (47%). A new question about self-reported ability in Irish revealed that 195,029 or 10 per cent of the total number of speakers reported speaking Irish very well and 593,898 or 32 per cent reported speaking Irish well. In terms of frequency of use, 115,065 or 2.3 per cent said that they spoke Irish weekly outside the education system, an increase of 3.2 per cent and 71,968 or 1.4 per cent reported speaking it every day both within and outside the education system, a drop of 2.5 per cent. In the historically Irish-speaking Gaeltacht areas, 65,156 people or 66.3 per cent indicated that they could speak Irish, an increase of 2.3 per cent from 2016. However, only 20,261 people or 19.7 per cent of the population reported speaking Irish every day, a drop of 1.6% on the previous census. However, this figure masks considerable differences between different areas where Irish may be weak or strong as a community language (Central Statistics Office, 2017 & 2022).[2]

In Northern Ireland, 228,600 people or 12.4 per cent of the population aged three and over reported some ability in the Irish language in the 2021 census, an increase from 2011. Within the population, 126,700 or 6.9 per cent said that they could speak Irish with 43,500 or 2.4 per cent doing so every day. Asked to record their 'main language', Irish was the third largest option after English, with 0.3 per cent of respondents (6,000 people) choosing that option (Northern Ireland Statistics and Research Agency, 2022a & 2022b). Although all six counties of Northern Ireland contained the vestiges of Gaeltacht areas when it was established in 1921, no such community survived the twentieth century. Irish language networks in Co Derry and in west Belfast have been recognised by Foras na Gaeilge, the cross-border agency for the Irish language set up under the Good Friday Agreement of 1998 (Walsh, 2022: 29–34).

Background

When the Irish state was established in 1922, a key policy plank was the revival of the Irish language throughout the country and the maintenance of Irish as the

---

[1] See, for instance, the Turas project based in east Belfast: https://www.cairdeturas.com/.
[2] I thank the census division of the Central Statistics Office for further assistance with this information.

primary language of the Gaeltacht, the scattered, mostly coastal, districts in the west that were historically Irish-speaking. Irish society and political culture were deeply conservative for most of the twentieth century and language policy was implemented in parallel with a raft of social policies that were strongly influenced by the Catholic Church (Walsh, 2022). This led to associations between the Irish language and conservative ideology, as outlined by one of the founders of AerachAiteachGaelach[3], who described the rationale for founding the group and staging the play *Idir Mise agus Craiceann do Chluaise*[4] in 2021:

> Tá sé an-tábhachtach dúinne cur i gcoinne an smaoinimh nach féidir dlúthbhaint a bheith idir Éireannachas/Gaelachas agus aiteacht. Sin rud ba mhaith linn a dhéanamh leis an ngrúpa seo agus le léiriú an dráma seo – is cuid den scéal náisiúnta é an scéal seo faoi dhaoine aiteacha (Ní É & McEvoy, 2021: 267).

> *It is very important for us to oppose the idea that there cannot be a close connection between Irishness/Irish speaking identity and queerness. That's what we want to do with this group and with the production of this play – this story about queer people is part of the national story* (translation).

This statement echoed research that I have been doing for some years about queer Irish speakers and it reminded me of the tension that some participants felt between identity related to the Irish language and identity related to their sexuality. On the one hand, the historical burden of conservatism was associated with the Irish language after the establishment of the state and it was believed that a trace of that ideology persisted. Various minorities who did not fit the hegemonic version of identity, including LGBTQ+ people, had been marginalised over the decades. On the other hand, English was strongly linked with global queer culture (Motschenbacher, 2011: 163) and there were concerns about the expression of sexuality in other languages, especially minority languages such as Irish. Some of the interviewees felt trapped between the global culture of the English language, on the one hand, and the historical conservative Irish culture, on the other hand (Walsh, 2019). It could be argued that there is a great diversity of opinion in the Irish community, that it has always contained a progressive strand, and that the people who spoke to me were not representative of the majority's experience. However, that was not the purpose of the research: what I set out to do was to conduct an initial investigation of opinions about such issues among a sample of people who felt some kind of belonging to

---

[3] See a description of the background to and activities of the group at https://www.aerachaiteach gaelach.net/ (Irish only).

[4] This translates literally as 'Between me and the skin of your ear', an idiom meaning that a person carrying a secret whispers it to someone else.

the 'Irish language community', however vague and uncertain that concept is. It was high time, in my opinion, to carry out social research on the identities of Irish-speaking queer people and my experience as a gay man whose coming-out story was linked to becoming a speaker of Irish was a strong personal motivation.

A leading historian of modern Irish history referred to a similar dynamic to that identified when he argued that many public intellectuals in the last century associated Irish language policy with a censorious and anti-intellectual official culture that was firmly rooted in the Catholic Church. Although some criticism of the Irish-speaking community was excessive and unfair, according to Gearóid Ó Tuathaigh (2011: 83) it was 'unfortunate' for the language that it was linked to conservatism and narrowness in the minds of progressive people in the past. There are many examples of that hostility in the public and intellectual discourse during the twentieth century and although Irish speakers were often unfairly and inaccurately stereotyped, such views gained a foothold in the public imagination and were a significant obstacle to the promotion of Irish over the years.

In the 2021 interview, Eoin McEvoy and his co-founder Ciara Ní É said that AerachAiteachGaelach aimed to challenge such understandings and provide a space where artists of all kinds could come together through the Irish language (Ní É, & McEvoy, 2021: 263). In that way, it would be possible to tackle the void felt by those who wish to practise both Irish language and queer identities. In an interview with me in 2022, both drew strongly on a language revitalisation discourse and said that it was important that AerachAiteachGaelach attracted artists to continue working in Irish rather than returning to English. They also used the label 'new speaker' to describe themselves and McEvoy emphasised the similarities between 'coming out' as a queer person and the conscious effort people make to become new speakers (McEvoy & Ní É, 2022). The 'new speaker' concept has been proposed as a lens through which to understand people who speak languages with which they do not have historical associations or experiences of early socialisation, for instance, in their families or communities. It attempts to move beyond rigid categories of 'native' and 'non-native' speakers and proposes a framework of analysis that transcends categories of deficit that are long-established in linguistics and related academic strands. Work drawing on the new speaker framework over the past decade has analysed the practices, ideologies and trajectories of people adopting languages other than their initial language of socialisation or community (for an overview of the new speaker concept, see O'Rourke et al., 2015; for an analysis of new speakers of Irish, including people who identity as gay or queer, see O'Rourke & Walsh, 2020).

The remainder of this article consists of an analysis of the play referred to earlier in this section, *Idir Mise agus Craiceann do Chluaise*, which was staged in 2021 as part of the Dublin Fringe Theatre Festival. The discussion begins with an analysis of interviews with the writers and the protagonist and is followed by a textual analysis of extracts from the script that highlighted salient themes related to the link between language and sexuality. I will argue that the play brought together different strands of the complex relationship between national identity, the Irish language, and queerness and that the theme of migration was effectively used as an integral part of the Irish experience, especially at the end of the twentieth century. The play was based on the story of Alan Walpole, a musician and barber who emigrated as a youth in the 1980s to escape the homophobic atmosphere in Dublin. After emigrating to England, Alan decided to reconnect with the Irish language and took up language classes. When he returned permanently to Ireland in 2018, he registered with AerachAiteachGaelach where, he said, he could express both aspects of his identity. The founders of AerachAiteachGaelach decided that they would write the story of his life but as shown in the play, it was challenging for Alan to settle in Ireland again and the process involved both relief and heartache. Eoin McEvoy explained that the group wanted to show that the stories of queer people, many of whom had to leave Ireland, are an integral part of Irish history (Ní É & McEvoy, 2021: 267). He gave more information in an interview with me:

Is cuimhin linn fós b'fhéidir ruball na tréimhse sin. Ní raibh sé éasca orainne ach ní raibh sé pioc cosúil leis an rud a raibh seisean [Alan] i ngleic leis ach ní raibh sé éasca ach an oiread dúinne agus mar sin d'aithin muid an-chuid de na rudaí a raibh sé ag caint mar gheall orthu. Ach theastaigh uainn go dtuigfeadh daoine atá níos óige arís ná muid gur rud an-nua é go bhfuil na saoirsí seo againn agus go bhfuil an saol níos fearr (McEvoy & Ní É, 2022).

We still remember perhaps the tail of that period. It wasn't easy for us but it wasn't one bit like what he [Alan] *was dealing with but it wasn't easy for us either so we recognised a lot of what he was talking about. But we wanted people who are younger than us to understand that it is a very new thing to have these freedoms and that life is better now* (translation).

Regarding Alan Walpole's linguistic background, his family in Dublin did not speak Irish but according to his own account, he acquired a reasonable ability from schooling and additional summer periods in the Irish-speaking Gaeltacht areas, where many children attend immersion courses during school holidays. While in England, he started learning Irish again and took the European Certificate in Irish (*Teastas Eorpach na Gaeilge*) exams at B2 (upper intermediate) level. After joining AerachAiteachGaelach back in Ireland, he was interviewed bilingually by the founders about his life and an immersive audio installation was created in seven different spaces representing various periods of his life. Among them were Alan's family home, a barber's shop in Dublin, a gay nightclub and bedroom in London, his family kitchen, the Dublin gay bar The George during the marriage referendum in 2015, and his mother's home in recent years. All spaces were created in the social club of Conradh na Gaeilge, a centre used by the Irish-speaking community in Dublin. *Idir Mise agus Craiceann do Chluaise* was not a conventional piece of art in the sense that one would imagine a stage play: due to the restrictions of Covid-19, the audience had to walk through the spaces one person at a time and listen to a soundtrack that was a combination of Alan Walpole's voice as a narrator and specially composed music. The installation was in Irish but an English translation of the script was available in the venue for those with limited Irish or no ability in it.

When interviewed by me, Alan Walpole explained the tension he had historically felt between his national and Irish language identity and his identity as a gay man and described how he came across AerachAiteachGaelach after returning to Dublin:

> Chonaic mé fógra greamaithe ar an doras agus ar an bhfógra sin bhí 'Queercal Comhrá', grúpa daoine aeracha a bhí ann agus bhí Gaeilge acu ach dúirt mé liom féin '*Jesus* nach bhfuil sé sin iontach?' Tharla sé sin beagnach ceithre bliana ó shin, an chéad uair i mo shaol go raibh mé chomh háthasach an saghas fógra sin a léamh ach thug sé sin dóchas dom go mbeadh mé in ann bualadh suas le daoine cosúil liomsa agus go mbeimis in ann comhrá a dhéanamh i nGaeilge ... Chuir sé sin gliondar ar mo chroí ach fuair mé amach ar an bpointe boise nach raibh mórán Gaeilge agam [gáire] (Walpole, 2022).

> *I saw a notice stuck on the door and on that notice was 'Queercal Comhrá',[5] it was a group of gay people and they spoke Irish but I said to myself 'Jesus isn't that great?' That happened almost four years ago, the first time in my life that I was so happy to read that kind of announcement but that gave me hope that I would be able to meet people like me and that we would be able to chat in Irish ... That made me really happy but I found out right away that I didn't know much Irish [laughter] (translation).*

Analysis of *Idir Mise agus Craiceann do Chluaise*

Three extracts from the play have been chosen for analysis in this section. The first captures the homophobia of Alan's youth before he emigrated, the second represents his elation during a visit home for the 2015 marriage equality

---

[5] Queercal Comhrá is a linguistic play on the term 'ciorcal comhrá' (conversation circle). This refers to the many informal Irish language conversation groups around the country.

referendum, and the third reflects his ambiguous feelings having returned home permanently in 2018. The play begins in his sitting room in 1980s Dublin where his parents condemn gay people while watching a television report on the AIDS crisis. Alan is outed when his mother reads his diary, describes him as 'very sick', and threatens to bring him to a psychiatrist. In the first extract, Alan tells us how this experience prompted him to decide to emigrate:

> Níl uaim fágáil ach cén rogha atá agam? Tá grá agam d'Éirinn ach níl grá aici dom. Nílim san áit cheart in Éirinn.
> [Guth na máthar:] *You are not, you are not, you are not.*
> Thaispeáin leaid éigin cóip de *The Gay Times* dom is mé amuigh ag damhsa in Flikkers. Agus mé ag féachaint tríd ar na fir dhathúla ag damhsa, iad saor, sásta, gan léinte orthu thall i Londain, arsa mise liom féin: 'Céard sa tsioc atá á dhéanamh anseo agam?'
> Deir Mam go bhfuil sí ag guí nach n-imeoidh mé. Tá sí buartha fúm – áit éigin in íochtar a croí. Ach caithfidh mé imeacht. Le mé féin a tharrtháil.
> Fág an tír sin nár ghlac ariamh leat. Téigh suas an pasáiste i dtreo do thodhchaí. Éalaigh liom is imigh liom ón oileán sin a mhúch tú. Siúil, siúil. Lean an ceol, lean do chosa, trasna na farraige. Teith liom. Go Sasana.
> [*Ceol: 'Upbeat X Fill a Rún', meascán idir port le hAries Beats agus amhrán Aoife Ní Mhórdha a rinneadh go speisialta don dráma*] (McEvoy & Ní É, 2021).

> *I don't want to leave but what choice do I have? I love Ireland but it doesn't love me. I'm not in the right place in Ireland.*
> [Mother's voice in English:] You are not, you are not, you are not.
> *A lad showed me a copy of* The Gay Times *while I was out dancing in Flikkers. As I looked through it at the handsome men dancing, free, happy, shirtless over in London, I said to myself: 'What the hell am I doing here?' Mam says she's praying that I won't go. She's worried about me – somewhere deep in her heart. But I have to go. To save myself.*
> *Leave that country that never accepted you. Walk up the aisle towards your future. Escape with me and depart with me from that island that suffocated you. Walk, walk. Follow the music, follow your feet, across the sea. Run away with me to England.*
> [*Music: 'Upbeat X Fill a Rún', a mix of a tune by Aries Beats and a song by Aoife Ní Mhórdha composed especially for the play*] (translation).

We see some of the tension between identities here: although Alan Walpole 'loves' Ireland, he feels completely out of place in it. Ireland is a suffocating country for him and he must flee to save himself. His mother adds to that alienation and the decision to recite her words in English creates a gap in the audience's mind between Alan and her. Flikkers was Dublin's gay club, based in the Hirschfeld Centre in Temple Bar until it burned to the ground in 1988. The use of music is very effective: the song 'Upbeat X Fill a Rún', a track specially composed for the play, is a mix of the traditional *sean-nós* style of unaccompanied Irish singing and synth-pop or new wave music of the 1980s.

The play then moves to London and the audience enters a gay nightclub and goes into Alan's bedroom. In a space containing the family kitchen table, the listener is told about a painful visit home by Alan with his new lover, Tony, in the 1990s. His parents denied them recognition as a couple by prohibiting any displays of affection and putting them in separate bedrooms. Later in the play, Alan describes a happier trip that he made to Ireland in 2015 for the marriage referendum:

> Téimis go hÉirinn le chéile. Lean an téip, siúil tríd an doras.
> [*Láithreán: Cóisir mhór ag Pantibar, dathanna, bratacha i ngach áit.*]
> An bhfeiceann tú na dathanna?
> [*Ceol: Retro Electro EDM le hAries Beats*]
> Cas timpeall, cas arís, cas is cas, luasc timpeall is timpeall, lig dóibh meascadh romhat: dearg, oráiste, buí, glas, gorm, corcra, bándearg, bánghorm, donn, dubh. Cá bhfuil tú? Tá tú in Éirinn. Sa bhaile! Fillte. Suigh in airde ar an stól. An difríocht atá ann! An meon. Athraithe go huile is go hiomlán. Ní chreidim gurb é an saol céanna é, gurb é an domhan céanna é. Éire athraithe. Tír a vótáil 'tá for grá'.
> GLÓR OIFIGIÚIL: Líon na vótaí i bhfabhar an togra: milliún, dhá chéad is a haon míle, sé chéad agus a seacht.
> [*Fuaim: Slua ag ceiliúradh go glórach. Tagann deireadh leis an gceol.*]
> (McEvoy & Ní É, 2021).

> *Let's go to Ireland together. Follow the tape, walk through the door.*
> [*Site: Big party at Pantibar,[6] colours, flags everywhere.*]
> *Do you see the colours?*
> [*Music: Retro Electro EDM by Aries Beats*]
>
> *Turn around, turn again, turn and turn, swing around and around, let them mix before you: red, orange, yellow, green, blue, purple, pink, white, brown, black. Where are you? You are in Ireland. At home! Returned. Sit up on the stool. What a difference! The mood. Completely changed. I don't believe it's the same world, it's the same world. A changed Ireland. A country that voted 'tá for grá'.[7]*
> OFFICIAL VOICE: *Number of votes in favour of the proposal: one million, two hundred and one thousand, six hundred and seven.*
> [*Sound: Crowd celebrating loudly. Music ends*] (McEvoy & Ní É, 2021).

---

[6] Popular gay bar in Dublin.

[7] A mixture of Irish and English meaning 'yes for love'. This slogan was used regularly by campaigners for the referendum, reflecting widespread passive knowledge of Irish among the general population due to years of exposure at school. There is no direct equivalent of 'yes' or 'no' in Irish as the relevant verb must be used instead. 'Tá' is the present tense of the verb 'to be' and is used to denote 'yes' in referendum questions. 'Grá' is the Irish for love.

In this extract, Alan shows his amazement at the result of the referendum, a public response that echoed the huge social change that took place in Ireland since he left years before. That transformation was incredible for him in light of what he suffered in his youth. Clever use is made of the country's official bilingualism by including the Irish part of the declaration of the referendum result on the sound-track. The Irish language is rarely mentioned explicitly in *Idir Mise* but because Alan made a conscious decision to tell the story of his life in that language, the chosen medium has profound symbolic importance. One reference to his learning journey is made in the play when Alan mentions a time when he was waiting for friends from the Queercal Comhrá in Pantibar. He called them 'my tribe' (*mo threibh*), an expression of the solidarity and belonging he felt with them.

The final passage to be discussed relates to the end of the play, where the story is told from 2018 onwards when Alan decided to return to Ireland on a long-term basis. At home again in the house where he was raised, he has mixed feelings because his mother still refuses to accept him as a gay man, but there is a glimmer of hope nonetheless:

> Mar gach ábhar díomá i mo shaol, d'eascair sé as an rud seo: gur fear aerach Éireannach mé. Ach gach cúis áthais freisin, tá a fhréamh sa rud céanna, gur fear aerach Éireannach mé, ar ais in Éirinn nua.
> Cá mbeidh mo thriall nuair a chaillfear Mam? Níl a fhios agam. Ach táim beo.
> [*Ceol: 'Upbeat X Fill a Rún' arís.*]
> Agus tá an t-ádh liom bheith beo. Tuigim sin. Táim fós chomh folláin leis an mbradán seang. Tá mo chroí fós lán de ghrá, de ghnéas, de mhianta. Ach ní raibh mé riamh in ann mé féin a chur in iúl mar is ceart. Go dtí anois.
> Tá cogadh mór fada buaite agam inniu. Má fhanaim, nó má fhillim thar farraige, táim ábalta labhairt faoi na rudaí seo ar deireadh. Leatsa (McEvoy & Ní É, 2021).

> *Like all disappointments in my life, it stemmed from this: that I was a gay Irish man. But every reason for joy is also rooted in the same thing, that I am an gay Irish man, back in the new Ireland.*
> *Where will I go when Mam dies? I don't know. But I'm alive.*
> [*Music: 'Upbeat X Fill a Rún' again.*]
> *And I'm lucky to be alive. I understand that. I'm still as fit as a fiddle. My heart is still full of love, sex, desires. But I was never able to express myself properly. Until now.*
> *I have won a great long war today. If I stay, or go abroad again, I'm able to talk about these things at last. With you* (translation).

In this passage, Alan tries to reconcile the rejection he experienced as a young man from Irish society (and to this day from his mother) and the comfort he found in a country that changed profoundly and to which he returned recently on a long-term basis. The essence of the solution is that he can express himself as both an Irishman and a gay man, which he could not do before. He still has an appetite for life, love, and sex, his health is good and wherever in the world he goes in the future, Alan is happy that he can finally speak publicly about both sides of his identity.

Reference was made earlier to Alan's trajectory with Irish from his school years in Ireland to taking Irish courses as an adult while living in Britain. It became clear to me as I walked through the various spaces of the installation that the soundtrack itself reflected a linguistic journey. On the soundtrack, it seemed that Alan started out slowly and hesitantly in Irish but that he gained courage linguistically as he moved through the story until, by the end of the play, I sensed his greater confidence and authority in his linguistic performance. The vast majority of the script is in Irish apart from some words in English attributed to his mother, the television report about AIDS, and jargon related to gay life or popular culture such as 'string vest', 'poppers', 'preppy', and 'catwalk'. I was keen to understand Alan's decision to tell his story in Irish, particularly because he had told me that he was far from comfortable in it when interviewed by AerachAiteachGaelach after his return to Ireland. Was it because he wanted to keep his story a secret from family members who did not speak Irish?

> Ní rud rúnda atá i gceist in aon chor. Ní hea – tá mé chomh bródúil go bhfuil sé i nGaeilge agus b'fhéidir mar gheall ar an mionphobal, b'fhéidir gurb in an fáth go gcuireann sé an méid sin gliondair ar mo chroí. Bhí mé in ann an mionphobal a shroisint, sea, mar sin tá sé déanta i nGaeilge (Walpole, 2022).

> *It's not a secret at all. No – I'm so proud that it's in Irish and maybe because of the minority community, maybe that's why it makes me so happy. I was able to reach the minority community, yes, so it's done in Irish* (translation).

Therefore, the decision to tell his story in Irish was conscious and aimed at making an impact on the Irish language community, a community in which Alan had participated openly as a gay man for the first time since his return to Ireland. The linguistic choice can also be read as an act of opposition: the use of Irish as a queer, subversive language and the challenging of the historical connection between the language and conservatism both in Alan's life and in society generally. Through the emotional distance that the Irish language provides, the linguistic choice helps Alan – and indeed many of the audience – to deal with the historical trauma of being queer in Ireland and the migration that was and still is an integral part of that experience. It is a new 'coming-out' story, not only by a gay man but an Irishman and a new speaker of Irish also. This groundbreaking audio installation does identity across time and space and underlines the importance of AerachAiteachGaelach as a space where queer Irish speakers can explore linguistic and sexual identities through the arts. This dynamic is summed up accurately by Eoin McEvoy:

Tá an t-imeall ann, agus tá an lár ann, agus ansin tá an tríú spás ann, áit ina dtógann tú an t-imeall agus ina ndéanann tú lár nua de. Deirtear sin faoin stáitse, mar shampla, ach braithim go bhfuil sé tarlaithe le hAerachAiteachGaelach mar go bhfuil muid théis a rá, 'Seo é anois. Seo é ár spás. Tá spás ann dúinn.' Agus má tá tú páirteach sa spás sin, is ionann sin agus an domhan duit, más maith leat, chomh maith le pé domhan eile atá agat (Ní É & McEvoy, 2021: 268).

There is the fringe and the centre and then there is the third space, where you take the fringe and you make it into a new centre. That is said about the stage, for instance, but I feel that it has happened with AerachAiteachGaelach because we have said, 'This is it now. This is our space. There is a space for us.' And if you are involved in that space, that is your world, if you like, along with whatever other world that you have (translation).

Following almost a century of official exclusion of queer people from the revitalisation of Irish, the work of AerachAiteachGaelach represents a vibrant and fluid space where Irish speakers can come together to create and share artistic material among themselves and in wider Irish-speaking networks. Its participatory ethos welcomes Irish speakers from different backgrounds, of varying levels of competence and representing a range of gender identities, and the trajectories of members often involve embracing both Irish and queerness at the same time. While operating on a voluntary and non-profit basis, AerachAiteachGaelach has received occasional funding from Foras na Gaeilge and has been included in various Irish language events that are funded indirectly from the same source, meaning that it has benefited from direct state support. *Idir Mise agus Craiceann do Chluaise* is an example of one of the group's initiatives to make Irish-language queerness more visible, recognising its transnational nature and the changing contours of Irish society. Representing an important strand of language revitalisation, the play underlines how queer people can integrate into Irish-speaking networks even if they face linguistic challenges, and it reconciles the processes of becoming a new speaker and realising a queer identity.

Making Breton Gender- and LGBTQIA+-Fair: Typographical and Lexical Expansion to Reflect Diversity within the Breton-Speaking Community

Michael Hornsby

Introduction

Celtic language communities, due to their proximity to and influence from the Anglo- and Francophone words, are just as much subject to tensions between conservative and modernising tendencies in majority language communities. In a similar fashion, these tensions between such tendencies can manifest in political, social, and, of course, linguistic outcomes. Boudreau (2016) has formulated three main types of discursive responsive to language minoritisation: traditionalist, modernising, and globalising. While these themes were initially identified in a Canadian context, Boudreau (2016: 152) points out how they are to be found in other minority language communities. As an analytical tool, they can be deemed useful for the present study, which focuses on lexical innovation within the Breton-speaking community. Many tensions can be identified in minority language communities that relate back to one or more of these discursive responses. The traditionalist discourse relies on the notion of a homogenous collectivity among minority language speakers and is tightly bound to linguistic conservatism; with the emphasis on native cultural reproduction (Boudreau, 2016: 151), a community is 'reimagined' by reference to its past (Heller & Labrie, 2003: 16). The modernising discourse in minority language communities, on the other hand, can rely on political structures – the minority is 'legitimate' and is entitled to accessing 'legitimate rights'. From a sociolinguistic point of view, the emphasis is on reforming the minority language, making it fit for modern life (Boudreau, 2016: 152). Modernising tendencies also involve 'reimagining' the minority community, but in contrast to the traditionalising discourse, the reimagination follows modern lines, in order to display ethnonational identity markers within wider collective identities (Heller & Labrie, 2003: 19). Finally, within a globalising discourse, the economy acts as a key domain within the valorisation of language forms and practices, and bilingualism, in whatever form, allows access to the benefits of globalisation and participation in the new economy (Boudreau, 2016: 152).

In this section, I discuss how the community of Breton speakers is engaging in 'modernising' practices in one particular scenario, through a number of marked linguistic forms related not only to gender-fair language but also LGBTQIA+-affirming language as well. Since gender/LGBTQIA+-fair language can be contested by some segments of the Breton-speaking population, this opposition is mentioned briefly in the later sections of this section. By way of an example of an initiative involving Breton speakers working on gender/LGBTQIA+-fair terms, a case study is included on the production of a lexicon by Difenn, a feminist organisation the membership of which has a sizeable proportion of Breton speakers. Finally, while the development of non-binary pronouns (a logical outcome of gender-neutral language planning) in Breton is not particularly advanced, this section nevertheless includes a brief discussion on representing non-binarity in the Breton language, an issue which appears to require further consideration in this particular context. This contrasts significantly with other situations of language minoritisation where the development of non-binary pronouns is much more advanced (see Daussà & Pera-Ros, this Element).

Sociolinguistic Background

Many minoritised language communities, including the Breton-speaking community, are understandably concerned with language revitalisation efforts to ensure the continuation of the language into the future. Breton revitalisers have quite a task on their hands: from a recorded high of 60 per cent of the total population of Brittany in 1886, the percentage of Breton speakers had dropped to just 5.9 per cent in 2009 (discussed in Hornsby, 2015: 19). A good proportion of speakers are aged seventy-five or older (46 per cent of the total Breton-speaking population in 2007), and younger speakers (under 24) make up just 4 per cent of the speaker population (Broudic, 2009: 66). The mode of transmission of Breton has been completely reversed between the younger and older generations: while nine out of ten of those over seventy acquired it from their parents, nine out of ten of the younger generation (under 24) learnt the language in an educational setting. Despite this rather dramatic reversal in transmission modes, it should further be noted that immersion in the local community (10 per cent) remains a significant mode of transmission of Breton (Chantreau & Moal, 2022: 80).

The small but growing community of younger 'new speakers' of Breton show differences between the type of Breton they speak and that of the 'traditional' Breton of older speakers (see Hornsby, 2017; Hornsby, 2019b). This is largely because, as a result of the gap in intergenerational transmission, these new speakers generally acquire a standardised variety, which differs from the regional variation apparent in traditional varieties; their linguistic output is also more susceptible to interference from French (Kennard, 2022: 248). Such speakers have been characterised as highly engaged in community and social efforts and young, active speakers are visible and influential in Brittany, as elsewhere in minoritised settings (e.g. Dołowy-Rybińska, 2020: 19).

One activity that some new speakers engage in are attempts to produce deliberately egalitarian forms in Breton, which can be linked to a particular language ideology encompassing feminist/egalitarian principles and a broadly left-wing political stance. Standardised orthography tends to be used in such attempts (though not exclusively so) and this can be linked to the acquisition of Breton by many new speakers early on in Breton-medium education, where such orthography will be routinely used. Such education is provided by a number of organisations in Brittany, which either emphasise immersion in Breton, with French being gradually introduced, or in bilingual streams in state or Catholic schools where pupils receive equal amounts of Breton and French and learn to read and write in French before Breton is introduced (Kennard, 2022: 249). Around 20,000 pupils in Brittany attend Breton-medium schooling (Ofis publik ar Brezhoneg, 2022: 17).

The Need for Better Representation in Language

For some Breton speakers, there is the feeling that all speakers of the language should be represented and that it is no longer acceptable to live 'in silence', as it were. While linguistics has traditionally presented language opaquely in an attempt at neutrality (most notably in the attempt to present masculine forms as all-inclusive), this is no longer felt to be sufficient for some in the Breton-speaking community, who seek a better and more equal 'distribution of speech' (Tevanian & Tissor, 2010: 15, my translation). In doing so, some Breton speakers aim for a much fuller representation of all who engage in the Breton-language community, and to acknowledge, in particular, the contribution women play in sustaining and developing this same community. In this framework, the female presence needs to be clearly reflected through and within language practices themselves; furthermore, by doing so, this development also gives those Breton speakers who wish to 'make things perfectly queer' to paraphrase Alexander Doty (1993), an opportunity to voice their opposition to heteronormativity in Breton-speaking circles.

Arguments against the use of inclusive orthography in Breton have been voiced and are discussed later in more detail. The arguments against its use are already well-known in French and include its supposedly 'ugly' nature (despite the same arguments having been used in opposition to the use of (semi-) colons and the cedilla, all of which provoked quite bitter debates when introduced into French (Viennot, 2018: 115). Another point sometimes raised about inclusive orthography is its supposed illegibility and lack of pronounceability, but these points have been successfully challenged by Gygax & Gesto (2007), among others, who have claimed that these factors are not impacted to any significant degree by inclusive writing. That inclusive language is 'ineffective' has been further challenged by Viennot (2018: 116), who claims that, in fact, it helps increase the visibility of women in the workforce. Another interesting argument put forward in defence of the use of inclusive writing, and one which is of particular relevance for Breton, is that it helps revitalise a language since it contributes to the language's development and modernisation. Overall, while inequalities in society are not caused by language itself (language merely reflects such inequalities), a more inclusive way of writing is still an important step toward the reduction of inequalities in society (Viennot, 2018: 124).

Modernisation of the Breton Language

The themes identified by Boudreau (2016: 148) are located within a framework of language as a social practice. As a social practice, language is used by its speakers to provide sites for its use which 'are often created by the speakers themselves, and often, it is in these invented spaces, in these intersections, that minoritised speakers find a place to express themselves' (Boudreau & Dubois, 2005: 186). The modernisation and standardisation of the Breton language has been an activity that Breton revitalisers have engaged in for more than a century now. The association Gwalarn, active in the second quarter of the twentieth century, adopted a purist approach in selecting literary vocabulary and in avoiding loanwords from French in its attempts to establish a modern literary tradition in Breton (Abalain, 1989: 198). Efforts by the Diwan school network in 1977, as the first immersion-style school system ever to use Breton as the medium of instruction, were needed to expand and elaborate existing terminology for its pupils. In addition to terminological development, the network has continued to further codify the language to a certain extent and to act as a force for normalisation at the same time. Thirdly, the Ofis publik ar Brezhoneg (literally 'public office of Breton'), established in 1999, acts as a semi-official language academy for Breton and publishes, among other things, booklets of vocabulary on specific domains, in order to expand the modern lexical field in Breton (Ar Rouz, 2016: 148).

From a LGBTQIA+ perspective, this modernising approach allows speakers to create spaces which allow greater and wider representations of members of the Breton language community in ways which had not been previously imagined. An example of an attempt to redress the balance in Breton culture has been at least one workshop to 'rework' the lyrics of traditional songs, in order to make them gender-fair and more relatable to modern life.

On 20th February 2016, the association DiReizh/En Tous Genres held a workshop, which was advertised in the following way:

(Ad)skrivañ pozioù[8]
Alies-mat e vez douget stereotipoù pe talvoudoù moral ha n'int ket mat dimp e- barzh ar c'hanaouennoù festoù-noz. Tost int dimp d'afer se ha droed 'meump da adperc'hennañ ar pleustroù poblek-se. Fellout a ra dimp lakaat anezhe da vevañ dre hon taolioù-arnod, en ur cheñch pozioù 'zo peotramant en ur c'hrouiñ reoù nevez-flamm! Deuit 'ta da skrivañ ho istorioù, ho troioù fall ha da rannañ anezhe dre ar c'han !

(Re)writing lyrics
The repertoire sung in *festoù-noz*[9] often carries stereotypes and moral values that do not mean much to us. We hold on to these practices despite everything and we have the right to reclaim these popular songs. We want to bring them to life through our experiences, by modifying existing texts or by creating new ones. Come and write your stories, your troubles and share them in song! [Translation mine]

---

[8] https://direizh.files.wordpress.com/2018/05/fly-direizh2finale.pdf.
[9] Plural of *fest-noz*, a traditional Breton cultural gathering with music and song.

For the organisers of this workshop, the modernisation of Breton involves challenging stereotypes perpetuated through traditional song, which often assign a secondary role to women, or which reinforce heteronormativity. They assert their right to engage with these songs, but on their own terms, by bringing in the contemporary experiences of the workshop participants and reflect society's more open attitude to non-traditional relationships than was the case in the past. From a sociolinguistic point of view, the modernisation of a minority language emphasises the need for reform, for making the language fit for modern life (Boudreau, 2016: 152). It also involves 'reimagining' the minority community along modern lines, in order to display ethnonational identity markers within wider collective identities (Heller & Labrie, 2003: 19). One reimagination of the Breton community is for it to be more inclusive of the range of all the speakers it encompasses, and in line with developments elsewhere, to focus on acknowledging the power differentials and dynamics in society and their negative effects. Inclusive language can also help work toward creating cultures where people can feel free to be their fully authentic selves.

Such an approach does not sit well with all Breton speakers, of course, and opposition reflects political affiliations and personal language ideologies (as indeed does the decision to use egalitarian language in the first place). Tensions can arise between those who hold a 'traditionalist' view of language maintenance and those who seek to modernise the Breton language by including more inclusive forms than are traditionally used. The use of egalitarian language in Breton in a Facebook post (where I invited Breton speakers to take part in an online survey about their language practices for a project on community building among linguistic minorities) created a small backlash. The use of egalitarian language was openly mocked – 'you only have to read the title in order to realise it's a sociological survey' (as if there is something wrong with sociology) and it put off one person from replying ('If I had noticed I wouldn't have bothered responding . . .') Another commenter notes that the suffix '-x' should be added in order to include the non-binary, but it is addressed to the first person to mock the practice, so it would not appear to be in solidarity. Negative attitudes towards inclusive language are nothing new, of course, and can be found within minority language communities as much as they are to be found in majority language communities as well. Indeed, a negative attitude toward linguistic inclusivity is most likely to overlap across the linguistic repertoire of a multilingual speaker, and objections towards such new forms are likely to be raised by the same speaker in French as much as in Breton.

Reducing Gender Asymmetries in Breton

Not unsurprisingly, Breton follows previously established trends that have been employed in French for some time now. Abbou (2011) has examined a number of strategies in French at the typographic, morphosyntactic, lexical, and rhetorical levels; of particular interest here are the typographical techniques which she has noted. These include, among other techniques,

(1) the use of brackets: *les étudiant(e)s* 'RAD-students[=masc]+[(fem marker in brackets)]';

(2) replacing a letter which refers to gender with a neutral symbol: *tu l* vois* 'You see him/her [* replaces e (masc) or a (fem)]'; *m_partenaire*: 'my [_ replaces -on (masc) or -a (fem)] partner';

(3) Using the feminine form as the generic: *toutes les auditrices* 'all the members (fem) of the audience';

(4) reformulation to make the reference less gender specific: *supervision professorale* 'professorial supervision' instead of *supervision par le professeur* 'supervision by the professor (masc)';

(5) mixing masculine and feminine nouns and adjectives: *certains militantes* 'certain (masc) activists (fem)'; and

(6) the use of a suspended full stop: les *chanteur•se•s* 'RAD-singer•(fem suffix)•(pl. suffix)' (Abbou, 2011: 38).

This last use of a suspended full stop (also called an interpunct, or middle dot [·]) is the technique most frequently used in Breton where the writer wishes to signal inclusivity. Take, for example, the following phrase, extracted from the *fest-noz DiReizh*[10] website: *ni, gwregelour·ezed·ien a Vreizh* (we, feminists from Brittany), where the root word, 'gwregelour' (feminist, m.) has *ezed* (feminine plural marker) as the first suffix, and *-ien* (masculine plural marker) as the second, indicating priority for the feminine in this instance. Interestingly, the root itself is marked as masculine, but it can be surmised that the feminine singular ending, *-ez*, is subsumed in the feminine plural ending, *-ezed*. This stood out from the French-language practice on the same page (the text itself was bilingual), where dashes were used instead: '*nous, militant-e-s féministes breton-ne-s* (we, Breton feminist activists). Whereas this practice is in fairly common use now among some Breton speakers, the emphasis more recently has been on the development of specific vocabulary related to LGBTQIA+ issues, which is discussed in more detail in the following section.

---

[10] A literal translation is 'non-binary festival'. See https://festnozdireizh.wordpress.com (accessed 1 May 2023).

Case Study: Aerlin

Such attempts to reduce gender asymmetries in Breton are situated within a language ideology that encompasses feminist and egalitarian principles. Developments are particularly fruitful at the time of writing (2023), since Difenn, a feminist association in Quimper (Finistère), is producing a pocket lexicon in the Breton language, which lists words from both feminist and LGBTQIA+ vocabularies. The lexicon, entitled *Aerlin* ('unicorn'), aims is to 'reflect changes in society' (Geffard, 2022) by studying and creating words in the Breton language to include feminist and inclusive vocabulary. The trilingual lexicon (Breton, French and English) encompasses LGBTQIA+ people, that is, lesbian, gay, bisexual, queer, intersex, asexual people, and so on, and will the first of its kind in the Breton-speaking world. The aim of the lexicon is being fulfilled by collecting and creating words in Breton related to 'queer culture' which, according to one of the project participants, 'encompasses all political identities that deviate from the heterosexual norm and patriarchy. It's another way of looking at the couple, friendships, [and] relationships' (Geffard, 2022). The lexicon is being populated by classifying words into several categories, such as a section on law and justice and the theme of sexuality is also taken into account. This includes words such as 'kiss', 'making love', 'massage' or vocabulary that refers to sexual practices. The 'political' category is by far the most extensive. The need for the lexicon can be partly attributed to a boom in the Breton feminist movement, which 'allows us to have plenty of resources. Today there is a profusion of podcasts, articles, resources that allow you to open up about queer issues. I learn new words every week'. It also allows Bretons to reclaim their language and make it evolve along with the times (Geffard, 2022).

Another impetus for the development of the lexicon was the need to address the lack of such words in daily speech. While there is a growing number of small vocabularies published to expand the lexicon in Breton for modern needs (just under thirty of them have been published so far by the Ofis publik ar Brezhoneg[11], including DIY terms, banking, golf and football, to name just a few), to date none has been devoted to feminist and LGBTQIA+ themes. The intersection between these two groups for the development of a related set of vocabulary items is a natural link for the authors, since they saw no contradiction between the two political movements of Breton feminism and LGBTQIA+ rights.[12]

As with the development of inclusive writing more generally, the project can be located in a broadly left-wing frame of reference. The financing of the project

---

[11] See www.fr.brezhoneg.bzh/49-lexiques.htm for more details.
[12] This and the following paragraphs in this section are based on a personal communication with Morgane Bramoullé, one of the authors of the lexicon (22 March 2023).

was sought from funds provided by Ar Redadeg (a popular and festive relay race, whose sponsorship creates funding for diverse Breton-language projects). According to one of the authors, there has been a lot of interest in the prospective publication of the lexicon, at least in Breton-speaking networks the authors are engaged with. Comments tend to be made not in Breton but in French, and at times the content of these comments has not been factually accurate (i.e. ideologically driven statements which do not accurately reflect the form or proposed use of the word under question).

As already mentioned, categories have been established to which terms are allocated according to their meaning. These categories are populated by the reuse of already established words to give a new meaning (e.g. *iskis* originally meaning 'strange' but now used in the sense of 'queer') but also by employing Breton etymology to create new words (e.g. *heñvelreizhiad* as a direct translation of 'homosexual') The use of neologisms in Breton has been a subject of debate over the past few decades (see Hornsby & Quentel (2013) for more detail) but is by now a tried-and-tested technique for expanding the lexicon. Terms from English have been borrowed for use in Breton ('queer' as an alternative for *iskis*, for example), and furthermore, the Basque language has served as an inspiration for word creation.[13]

One technique the authors of the lexicon are keen to promote is the coining of portmanteau forms. A portmanteau is a single morph that is analysed as representing two (or more) underlying morphemes. The following portmanteau word, *selaouerienezed* 'listeners', is composed of the word 'listener' (*selaouer* m.sing.), plus the suffix -*ien* to denote the masculine plural (*selouerien*); the term is then feminised (-*ez*) and then pluralised in the feminine (-*ed*) to produce the portmanteau of *selaouer·ien·ez·ed*, which, while rather long, is still pronounceable. The term is in fact in actual use on Breton-language radio stations (alongside its French equivalent of *auditeurices*) and to date, the term has not been the subject of comment or contestation in public fora. It does, however, stand in contrast to the term for 'feminists' already referred to in the data from the *fest-noz DiReizh* website (*gwregelour·ezed·ien*) since the latter emphasises the feminine plural first and then the masculine plural. While both forms are long, they are identifiably morphologically Breton, even if they differ in the choice of the order of suffixes.

The portmanteau technique is particularly favoured by the authors of the lexicon, since not only can it include people's preferred gender expression but can also encompass non-binary people. This consideration was expressed

---

[13] For example, the Basque *tximeleta* meaning 'butterfly' has been adopted as the non-pejorative word for 'gay man' in lieu of the traditional and pejorative term *marikoi*, originating from the Spanish word *maricón* ('faggot').

earlier on in the section on modernisation, where one commentator proposed the incorporation of -x to express non-binarity, much in line with the word Latinx, which is an inclusive, non-gendered term for non-binary, gender-fluid, queer people of Latin American heritage in the United States of America. But since the letter does not exist in Breton, it is doubtful whether the commentator was sincere in their attempt to express solidarity with non-binary Breton speakers, unlike the authors of the Aerlen lexicon. Moreover, the use of the Latinx term in the USA, and its applicability for the rest of the Spanish-language domain, has subsequently been problematised since its introduction (see Daussà & Pera-Ros, this Element).

While the primary aim of the lexicon is to list vocabulary items of relevance to both Breton-speaking women and/or the Breton-speaking LGBTQIA+ community, another consideration the authors face is how to treat prepositions inclusively in Breton. Like other Celtic languages, prepositions and pronouns are combined when they are in direct proximity to each other, resulting in specific forms (*prepositional* pronouns) as a result, which can be gendered. For example, the preposition *da* 'to' is inflected as follows (in standard Breton):

1st pers. sing.	*din*	'to me'
2nd pers. sing.	*dit*	'to you'
3rd pers. sing. masc.	***dezhañ***	**'to him'**
3rd pers. sing. fem.	***dezhi***	**'to her'**
1st pers. pl.	*deomp*	'to us'
2nd pers. pl.	*deoc'h*	'to you'
3rd pers. pl.	*dezho* or *dezhe*	'to them'

The two third person singular forms ***dezhañ*** (masc.) and ***dezhi*** (fem.) forms are sometimes combined to ***dezhiañ*** to form an inclusive or non-binary form (pers. comm. Bramoullé, 22 March 2023).

Conclusion

The construction of a feminist and LGBTQIA+ lexicon goes some way toward moving dominant heteronormative discourses with Breton-speaking circles toward a more explicit critique of 'objective' and often unquestioned authority. Such authority can include precise, explicit norms, such as grammar rules, to more general, implicit and even unconscious socio-cultural norms related to heteronormativity. Though often overlooked and hardly ever openly mentioned, these social norms play a highly influential role in the processes of lexical elaboration and the current move toward more inclusive writing and vocabulary in Breton indicates a challenge to such social norms.

For a long time in Brittany, it has been a case of 'don't ask, don't tell', and in such an atmosphere, there was no need for specific terms to describe LGBTQIA+ Breton speakers, since such matters were not openly discussed. The tide appears to be turning in Brittany and there is now, more than ever, a perceived need to be more vocal about the presence of LGBTQIA+ Breton speakers within the language community. Issues of power and authority do not only influence lexico-graphical and typographical decisions in inclusive writing but are also produced by lexicons and gender-/LGBTQIA+-fair language themselves. As Breton-speakers seek greater and fairer representation in their language, grass roots efforts to effect such change can empower speakers to re-think linguistic, cultural, and social power structures. Queering lexical approaches to language change 'contributes to detecting structures of power and of heteronormative discourses in order to make them visible and raise awareness of their existence, a necessary first step in challenging them' (Nossem, 2017: 185). With this move to incorporating a queer approach more widely in the modernisation of the Breton language, feminist and/or LGBTQIA+ Breton speakers are enriching the base for future language revitalisation efforts. By doing so, these Breton speakers seek to create a refuge away from the dominant cultural sphere (Boudreau, 2016). So far, all indications seem to indicate little to no tension between feminist and LGBTQIA+ approaches to this matter in Breton-speaking circles. Opposition would seem to be more entrenched toward such modernising tendencies by more traditional-ist, non-feminist/non-LGBTQIA+ commentators, but according to Bramoullé, such opposition appears exclusively online rather than in real life (pers. comm. Bramoullé, 22 March 2023).

This is not to say, however, that other points of opposition will not arise as the situation in Brittany evolves. As in many other parts of the world, trans-exclusionary objections to representations of trans and non-binary people (in language and in other domains) is as prevalent in France as elsewhere, and while there is little evidence of this occurring in this particular setting at the present time, such dynamics are of course susceptible to change. As Caldwall (2018: 44) has noted, for those feminists who accept patriarchy theory, 'women are oppressed not because of the way that modern capitalism relies on the family for its own needs, but because of [their] role in the reproductive process per se. Biology trumps any socio-historical explanation of oppression, and men bene-fit from, or are privileged by, this oppression and thus have an interest in maintaining it'. Such an approach would result in the disruption of the current gender-fair developments occurring in Breton. The authors of the lexicon mentioned were keen to emphasise the intersectionality of LGBTQIA+ and feminist issues in their work. However, the appearance of publications such as *Fractures: Le féminisme et le mouvement LGBT en danger* (Le Doaré, 2021) points to a tendency to see an approach which emphasises the intersectionality between feminism and LGBTQIA+ issues as a threat:

> Le féminisme est aujourd'hui en danger, alors que son unité et ses fondamentaux sont violemment remis en cause par des activistes issus de courants de pensées identitaires et relativistes. Le mouvement LGBT, lui, se fracture en interne et ne représente plus guère les lesbiennes féministes (Le Doaré, 2021: back cover).

> Feminism is in danger today, while its unity and its fundamentals are being violently challenged by activists from identity and relativist currents of thought. The LGBT movement, on the other hand, is fracturing internally and perhaps no longer represents feminist lesbians (translation mine).

Therefore, it remains to be seen if such an understanding of the 'dangers' of intersectionality will become apparent in Breton-speaking circles, under the influence of French trans-exclusionary feminism, as the dynamics of gender-fair language in Breton develop, or if Breton feminists and/or LGBTQIA+ people in Brittany will continue to cultivate a uniquely Breton response to gender and sexuality equality in late modernity.

The Battle for Authority, Legitimacy, and Agency in the Twitter Fields of the Catalan Gender-Neutral Linguistic Revolution

Eva J. Daussà and Renée Pera-Ros

Introduction

When considering the relevance of the debate around gender-inclusive language on language vitality, Catalan presents an interesting case. At the ten million mark, it is a medium-sized linguistic community with a substantial presence both within its historical territory and internationally. However, due to global processes, together with unreliable institutional support, its vitality suffers to the point of being disproportionately under threat. Against this backdrop, it is interesting to examine its users' reaction to a linguistic innovation reflecting a societal debate, as it might have an impact on the viability of the language vis-à-vis satisfying its expressive and performative needs – the failure of which might add to its external pressures. In this section we examine Catalan's proposals for so-called gender-neutral language (GNL), and we focus on the attitudes and opinions around them as seen on Twitter (re-named as X in 2023 but referred to by its long-established name in this section). While some see GNL as a useful way to visibilise silenced identities and express one's commitment for social equality, others resist it on the grounds of linguistic authenticity (related to the threat of assimilation into Spanish or the advance of English), as well as questioning the legitimacy of linguistic agency and authority. Finally, we emphasise the cost of not adopting this international trend for a minoritised bilingual community that is ever on the verge of language shift.

Discussions of how language has an impact on the perception of reality regarding gender biases are not new (e.g. Lakoff, 1973; Penelope, 1988), and have more recently been confirmed experimentally (e.g. Boroditsky et al., 2003; Everett, 2011; Kaufmann and Bohner, 2014; Coady, 2018). On the other hand, evidence across languages seems to point to the effectiveness of more gender-neutral language (henceforth GNL, after Bonnin & Coronel, 2021) in reducing gender stereotyping and discrimination (Gustafsson Sendén et al., 2015; Sczensy et al., 2016; Brutt-Griffler & Kim, 2017; Shoham & Lee, 2018). For some individuals (notably, feminists, transgender, and gender-nonconforming or non-binary people), gender-neutral language offers a valuable opportunity to express and perform their gender identities beyond the rigid boundaries of traditionally binary and (heterocis-) normative linguistic structures (Zimman, 2018). Finally, the ability to grammatically and pragmatically accommodate GNL has also been interpreted as an index of linguistic vitality in the case of small or minoritised languages (Popic & Gorjanc, 2018; Hornsby, 2019a).

Under the labels of 'gender-fair', 'gender-inclusive', 'gender-neutral', 'non-gendered', 'non-binary', or 'non-sexist' language, the phenomenon is far from being a cultural peculiarity affecting a limited subset of languages, but rather it has spread widely among a large array of typologically diverse languages (Berger, 2019). This linguistic innovation is oftentimes surrounded by a heated politicised controversy, transparently mimicking the ways in which language is ever inter-dependent with social and institutional practices of discrimination and exclusion (Butler, 1990; Heller, 2007). The fact that some forms of GNL are making it to the mainstream indicates that GNL is unlikely to expire (Sánchez & Mayo, 2019). This is the case because it responds to a strong social will, or need, to visibilise *all* people, independent of their gender or sexual identification, and especially those individuals and communities that have been historically discriminated against (Parra & Serafini, 2022; Pennycook, 2017).

Well-established institutions bestowed with (official) authority on language matters vary in their attitude towards the phenomenon. For example, the American Dialect Society made headlines in choosing singular 'they' as 'word of the year' in 2015; that was the same year that Sweden saw the onset of the *hen revolution*, when after an initial objection, the gender-neutral neopronoun *hen* was included in the *Ordbok*, the comprehensive historical dictionary controlled by the Swedish Language Council. In contrast, the French Academy called GNL an 'aberration' (Académie française, 2017), and the Spain-based Real Academia Española (RAE) issued a strong rejection of (some forms of) GNL, dismissing it as a fashion and calling it 'unnecessary', 'alien to the Spanish language', and 'cumbersome' (Moretti, 2018) in spite of a widespread call for a more open-minded stance from the academic community (Ruiz Mantilla, 2020; del Valle, 2018; Sánchez & Mayo, 2019; Pérez & Moragas, 2020; cf. however, Nieves & Hernández, 2022, showing that the academic community does not agree on the topic either). Recently (although somewhat late to the debate), the *Institut d'Estudis Catalans*, with authority in the matters of Catalan, rejected some forms of gender-fair language in favour of the generic masculine, while it did not even acknowledge the existence of proposals (Moyano, 2023) of Catalan GNL that explicitly included non-binary identities (IEC, 2023).

On the ground, universities, private companies, local governments, and the like are increasingly issuing their own style guidelines for GNL, in an attempt to regulate a practice that seems to have taken a life of its own (Fuertes Gutiérrez, 2022). For example, there are some proposals designing tools to include GNL in language teaching (Parra & Serafini, 2021), and there is a new awareness towards moving beyond dichotomic gender categories in research design (Ansara & Hegarty, 2014), especially in fields where gender identity and biological sexuality might be taken for granted when using gendered language, for example, in laboratory tests and medical records (Imborek et al., 2017). Among the wider population, an extensive social network questionnaire surveying attitudes towards GNL and its adoption in Argentina (Bonnin & Coronel, 2021) found that even a favourable attitude of acceptance did not imply willingness to use it, regardless of gender identification. On the other hand, research based on Swedish had shown that, over time, initial resistance to gender-fair language shifts to positive attitudes and an increase in adoption (Gustafsson Sendén et al., 2015). This dynamism would mean that a continuous monitoring of the situation, taking various sources of data and domains into account, might be more indicative than one-shot snaps.

Against this backdrop, this section examines the linguistic attitudes surrounding the use of Catalan GNL as it concerns the so-called neo-pronouns and neo-morphemes, and as they are expressed in the social media open platform of Twitter. Discourse analysis studies of how gender identities are reflected in social media platforms abound (e.g. Milani, 2013; Bailey, 2019; Kalinowski, 2020), exploiting this relatively new source of naturalistic data for a variety of topics. With our study we would like to add to the knowledge pool from the perspective of Catalan GNL.

Catalan

With about ten million (bilingual) users, Catalan is a medium-sized Romance language (Plataforma per la Llengua, 2019). However, Catalan faces several serious challenges that endanger its vitality; for instance, relatively low social use and periodic hostile political attacks lead by pro-Spanish agents. Moreover, decades of ideologies undermining its everyday use have brought its speakers permanently to the verge of language shift (Vila, 2013). Among youth especially (Trenchs-Parera et al., 2014), where conceptions about languages and identities being multiple, fluid, and hybrid rather than unitary or immobile are especially entertained (Woolard & Frekko, 2013), multilingualism is embraced as a sign of cosmopolitanism, yet all too often these ideas manifest themselves in the shape of an eagerness to incorporate English to local linguistic repertoires which always include Spanish but not Catalan.

Catalan Neomorphemes and Neopronouns

Normative Catalan has a binary paradigm in its nominal gender system, differentiating masculine and feminine. These are traditional labels that go beyond sexed or gendered referents, but rather act as required grammatical classifiers for all nominal elements. Nouns, pronouns, adjectives, determiners, and some quantifiers are inflected and demand morphological agreement when sharing a referent. The masculine is the unmarked form, and oftentimes has no overt morpheme; the feminine takes the suffix [ə], written as < a > (or < e > in the plural, which is itself expressed by the suffix [s]), as can be seen in the following examples (where the determiner is *el* in masculine and *la* in feminine):

(1) El   fill   petit
     the.MASCULINE offspring.ø young.ø
     'the young(er) son'

(2) La   filla   petita
     the.FEMININE offspring.FEMININE young.FEMININE
     'the young(er) daughter'

(3) Tots
     all.ø.PLURAL
     'everyone' [masculine/generic]

(4) Totes
     all.FEMININE.PLURAL
     'everyone' [feminine]

(5) Els   meus   fills
     the.MASCULINE.PLURAL my.ø.PLURAL offspring,ø.PLURAL
     'my sons/my children'

(6) Les   meves   filles
     the.FEMININE.PLURAL my.FEMININE.PLURAL offspring.FEMININE.
     PLURAL
     'my daughters'

The most mainstream gender-fair proposal is reduplication (*els meus fills i les meves filles*, 'my sons and my daughters'), or the use of an epicene noun if there is one (*la canalla*, 'the children', which in spite of its feminine morphology has inclusive gender). The first option can become quite cumbersome, while the second one is lexically limited. A less frequent alternative is the use of generic feminine. It should be noted that all of these alternatives preserve gender binarism.

In their will to further overcome their linguistic gender bias, Catalan users have come up with a variety of GNL solutions. Following the early lead of Spanish, the first innovations (in the late 1990s and early 2000s) consisted of replacing the binary morphemes by < x > and < @ > (for example, *totxs* or *tot@s*). The former was associated with the Latinx community of the USA, and its applicability for the rest of the Spanish language domain, and by extension its Catalan counterpart, has since been problematised (Torres, 2018); the <@> graph, in turn, initially chosen because it graphically contained both the < o > and the < a > forms associated with the two traditional grammatical genders in Spanish, has also been questioned on the grounds of its binarism. Both forms, of course, share the hindrance that, while they work perfectly well in written text, they cannot be pronounced. In Spanish, the neomorpheme [e] was introduced, both in its phonetic and written forms. There is little data to evaluate the scope of the acceptance of each of these proposals in Spanish (*pace* Fundeu, 2020).

In our research we found the neomorpheme [i] (< i >) as the most popular variety of Catalan GNL. This form is generally built upon the feminine lexeme, completing the gender paradigm summarised earlier:

(7)   Li   filli
       the.GNL offspring.GNL
       'the child (of)'

(8)   Totis   lis   mevis   fillis
       all.GNL.PLURAL the.GNL.PLURAL my.GNL.PLURAL offspring.GNL.
       PLURAL
       'all my children'

The following examples from Twitter illustrate the most common usages of GNL, mainly to express a gender-neutral meaning for either a generic or a unspecified referent (Figure 2), to include all genders (Figure 3), as well as to signify a non-binary or gender-nonconforming identity (Figure 4).

Admittedly, this account constitutes a very simplified (even simplistic) picture of the morphological complexities caused by this innovation. In real life, a consistent adoption of GNL poses many challenges, some of them phonomorphological adaptations, and some introducing syntactic and semantic

Avui, tot i la nit del lloro que he passat, començo el dia amb notícies meravelloses!
Gràcies a totis lis que em vau enviar energia positiva la setmana passada!

12:16 p. m. · 13 de jul. de 2022 · Twitter for iPhone

Figure 2 (Second paragraph:) '*Thanks to all those who sent me positive energy last week*'.

Aquest nou semestre (i l'últim de la meva vida universitària) només vull veure a lis mevis amiguis, això és tot el que necessito

6:06 a. m. · 28 de jul. de 2022 · Twitter for iPhone

Figure 3 '*This new term (and the last one at university in my life) I just want to see my friends, this is all I need*'.

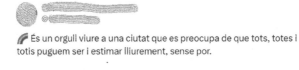

És un orgull viure a una ciutat que es preocupa de que tots, totes i totis puguem ser i estimar lliurement, sense por.

Gràcies @LorenRiderJ per l'empenta 💜

Figure 4 '*I'm proud to live in a city that makes sure that everyone* [tots, totes *and* totis] *can be free and love freely, with no fear*'.

ambiguities that undermine its very purpose. Faced with grammatical hesitation, some users adopt an avoidant strategy, resorting to duplications (or triplications) and epicene and mass nouns, while others venture innovative solutions. In this section we focus on the most extended proposal, which is the aforementioned neomorpheme $< i >$, and since our focus is set on the attitudes surrounding this linguistic innovation, we cluster together all of its meanings.

Methodology

This research was based on over 150 Twitter posts, produced between 21 March 2018 and 6 April 2023. Most tweets were found through purposive criterion sampling (Palys, 2008), in first instance by using key words in gender-neutral or non-binary language, such as 'totis' (*everyone*) and 'amiguis' (*friends*), and later under the keyword 'llenguatge inclusiu' (*inclusive lan-guage*). Additional tweets were found by chance, simply by scrolling down. The data was further restricted by eliminating re-tweets, tweets from the same person illustrating the same point, and relative cleanliness of the message (that is, it be written in legible form, with an aim to be in correct language, etc.). Profile information was checked in order to avoid tweets from institutions, political associations, news articles, and so on, as the emphasis was on the attitudes of individuals. At the theme analysis stage, once we had enough tweets to illustrate a point, we stopped collecting more items for it.

Tweets were observed for approximately one year prior to the data collection phase. They were captured individually or in the threads in which they were produced through a screen shot function, and they were numbered and stored individually. In spite of the data having public status (and being too short to create copyright issues), tweets are being anonymised for the purposes of presentation in this section. This is achieved by blurring profile names and pictures, and carefully excluding any personal data that could make the tweet easily recognisable.

In our study we followed the reflexive thematic analysis methodology outlined in Braun & Clarke, 2006 and Clarke & Braun, 2017, moreover following Kiger and Varpio's six-step process of data familiarisation, initial code generation, and searching, reviewing, defining, and naming themes (Kiger & Varpio, 2020). The naming of themes was furthermore influenced by theoretical ideas existing in the literature, such as those of legitimacy, purity, and authority in Woolard & Frekko (2013), Milroy (2001), Woolard (2016), and Heller (2006), as well as those reflecting the performative role of language (Butler, 1990). Because of limitations of space, the following section directly summarises our main findings, already defined and named, and includes only token illustrative tweets.

Results: Responses and Themes

Attitudes and responses expressed through Twitter showed a fair degree of polarisation between those that were positive and even enthusiastic, and those that were negative, mocking and opposing. After months of collecting tweets, we were left with the feeling that negative reactions had been easier to come across, although we did not have sufficient empirical grounds for a rigorous conclusive quantification. Among the reasons given for people's reactions and opinions, the majority could conceivably hold for GNL in any language, yet a few had a clearer link to the (sociolinguistic) peculiarity of Catalan.

The following paragraphs summarise the final classification of responses. We have divided them into positive and negative. We think that a more nuanced categorisation, with feelings potentially falling into a continuum between these radical reactions, is likely to be more representative of the debate, yet our research still yielded a robust polarisation between those who embraced and celebrated GNL and those who strongly rejected it. This could be an artefact of the medium of Twitter, where users are restricted in the number of characters within which to fit their opinions into a slogan-like summary that may not do them justice, and where a generalised climate of confrontation is commonly assumed or at least tolerated. Consequently, we have divided the responses into those that show a positive inclination (curiosity, interest, even enthusiasm; taking it as a reflection of an on-going social and cultural change worthy of attention), and those that show a negative reaction (showing resistance to change because of lack of familiarity, regarding GNL as an untimely fashion, ridiculing and mocking it, denying its effectiveness as a tool for social change, and even calling it an imposition by fake progressive groups).

Table 2 defines recurrent themes.

Table 2 Themes

Themes	Explanation
Authority	Whether there is a given entity, institution, or professional group that feels entitled to dictate the shape of a language.
Legitimacy	Whether the new forms are seen as belonging to the language or rather introducing impurities or disfiguring it.
Linguistic agency	Whether language users can exert necessary changes to make it serve their communicative and expressive needs.
Sub-themes	
Linguistic determinism	Whether language change has a role in social change; whether a social change should exert a linguistic change.
Performativity	Whether language can be used to represent and enact an individual or group identity.
Link with wider causes	Whether this is an issue linked to wider struggles for equality and social justice.
Language vitality	Whether GNL may have consequences for the vitality of the language.

Positive Attitudes

Perhaps the most tale-telling sign of a positive attitude is adoption (although recall Bonnin and Coronel's 2021 study indicating a lack of correlation in this respect). In Catalan, the use of GNL still signifies the will of going the extra mile in one's commitment to gender equality and inclusion. It is much less normalised than generic uses of the feminine or duplications, the latter being the most frequent recommendation in style guides and often seen in official billboards and texts. Our sense is that the use of the neomorpheme is far from being as widely used as, say, *singular them* in English, or even the equivalent morpheme in Spanish, something that we see confirmed in the fact that when it is used, more often than not it is cause for targeted comments.

In the vastness of Twitter, we found spaces for a fairly open debate about GNL, in which people made use of the medium to educate themselves on the topic, express their candid responses, and explore the phenomenon with curiosity. Questions and responses formulated in a polite and helpful way are appreciated (and retweeted; e.g. Figures 5 and 6), however, oftentimes until someone crashes the discussion with some kind of insult or other dismissive gesture (Figure 7).

Jo, de moment, no ho veig clar, però la Roqueta és l'única que trobo que explica les coses d'una forma entenedora i sense afectació. M'agrada i repiulo.

9:06 a. m. · 20 de març de 2021

Figure 5 '*It's not clear to me, for the time being, but I think that* [name of a person] *is the only one who explains things in an understanding and reasonable way. I like it and I'm retweeting it*'.

Entenc l'opció, però l'omissió no invisibilitza? És equivalent no expressar el gènere a ser de gènere no binari? Pregunto des del desconeixement i l'interès.

11:32 a. m. · 1 de febr. de 2022

Figure 6 '*I understand the alternative, but isn't omitting also invisibilising? Is not expressing one's gender equivalent to being non-binary? I'm asking out of lack of knowledge and interest*'.

En resposta a @⬛⬛⬛ i a @⬛⬛⬛
És un disbarat i una imposició. De català, no n'és gens.

Figure 7 '*I think it is nonsense and an imposition. It is in no way Catalan*'.

There are some openly positive reactions that go beyond pure acceptance, and even express some degree of enthusiasm; for example, in pointing out the gains of GNL in promoting visibilisation and inclusion:

Les persones de gènere no binari ho tenen molt més fàcil per referir-se a elles mateixes. Això ja és un salt!

6:51 p. m. · 11 d'ag. de 2018

Figure 8 '*It's much easier for non-binary people to refer to themselves. This is quite a jump* [forward]!'

The inclusion derived from the use of GNL is also linked to an increase in empathy:

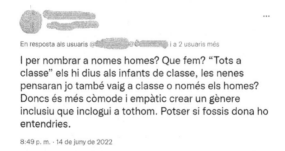

En resposta als usuaris @⬛⬛⬛ @⬛⬛⬛ i a 2 usuaris més

I per nombrar a nomes homes? Que fem? "Tots a classe" els hi dius als infants de classe, les nenes pensaran jo també vaig a classe o només els homes? Doncs és més còmode i empàtic crear un gènere inclusiu que inclogui a tothom. Potser si fossis dona ho entendries.

8:49 p. m. · 14 de juny de 2022

Figure 9 '*What about if we're referring to both men and women? What do we do? You tell the school children "All kids* [generic masculine]*: get into the classroom", girls will wonder if they should also go or only boys? So it's more convenient and empathetic to create an inclusive gender that includes everyone. Maybe if you were a woman you'd understand it*'.

The importance of the phenomenon is explained in terms of some version of linguistic determinism – changing language will bring about a change in society:

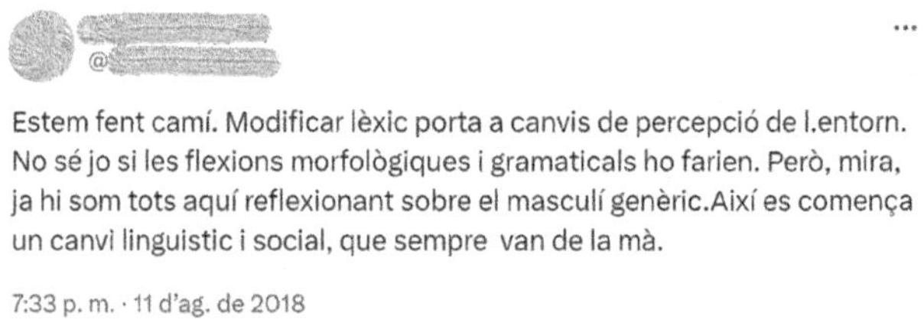

Estem fent camí. Modificar lèxic porta a canvis de percepció de l.entorn.
No sé jo si les flexions morfològiques i gramaticals ho farien. Però, mira,
ja hi som tots aquí reflexionant sobre el masculí genèric.Així es comença
un canvi linguistic i social, que sempre van de la mà.

7:33 p. m. · 11 d'ag. de 2018

Figure 10 '*We're making way. Modifying words changes the perception of the environment. I don't know whether morphological and grammatical inflection would do it. But look: here we all are debating about the generic masculine. This is how social and linguistic changes start, they always go hand in hand*'.

We see in these cases an ideology that emphasises the performative function of language, as well as the ability of language to enact identities and make individuals and groups visible. It intersects with the question of authority too, in the sense that the agency for linguistic shaping is given to the users of the language without waiting for an official blessing. It is remarked that the responsibility of professional linguists is to describe these developments, not to prescribe them:

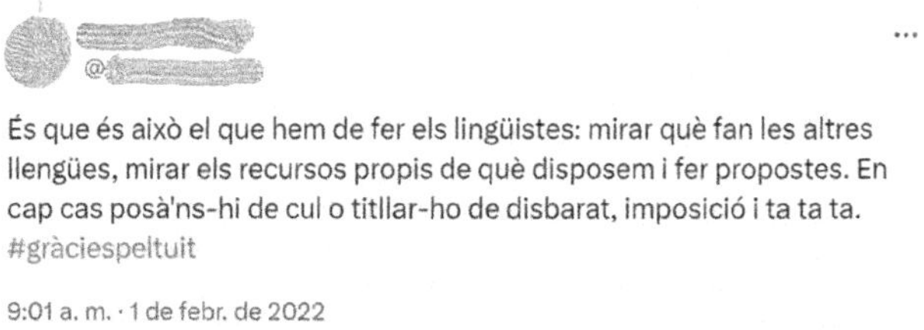

És que és això el que hem de fer els lingüistes: mirar què fan les altres
llengües, mirar els recursos propis de què disposem i fer propostes. En
cap cas posà'ns-hi de cul o titllar-ho de disbarat, imposició i ta ta ta.
#gràciespeltuit

9:01 a. m. · 1 de febr. de 2022

Figure 11 '*This is what we linguists have to do: observe what other languages do, check what resources our own language has and make suggestions. By no means should we reject it just because, or call it nonsense, imposition and blah-blah-blah*'.

The difficulty of dealing with an unfamiliar development is acknowledged, but it is not necessarily seen in negative light, even when things are not very clear:

Per la majoria que no estem acostumats a aquest tipus de llenguatge
encara ens sembla forçat. Com amb tantes coses, n'hem d'aprendre!

Tot i així, un dubte. Quan es fa servir el totis/todes, no inclou ja a
tothom?
És a dir, posar les tres formes no és una mica contradictori?

4:36 p. m. · 25 de set. de 2022

Figure 12 '*For those of us who are not used to this kind of language, it still sounds unnatural. Like so many other things, we need to learn*!'

Change is not always received with curiosity and openness though. Even those who are in principle accepting might cast their doubts about a generalised use, especially if there are alternatives:

Fa temps que ho llegeixo pel Twitter, aquest inclusiu en castellà de la 'e' i
fer el mateix en català però amb la 'i' m'agrada. Però sense abusar. Tenim
lèxic i formes de naturalesa inclusiva, com per exemple gent/persona
que és aplicable en qualsevol cas.

7:33 p. m. · 11 d'ag. de 2018

Figure 13 '*I've been reading this inclusive* [language] *in Twitter for a while; Spanish does it with -e and we do the same in Catalan but with -i. I like it. But we shouldn't abuse it. We have lexicon and forms which are already inclusive, for example people/person which is applicable to all cases.*'

Willingness to change sometimes comes with some negotiation, showing again a hierarchy of acceptance in the solutions against gender-biased practices:

Tinc dues filles i un fill més petit. Sóc incapaç de dir els meus fills, em
sembla que traeixo les noies, q ja hi eren,i eren,abans de néixer ell. Amb
elles, noproblem, el nen accepta el femení. Però quan parlo fora de casa
desdoblo el plural per fer-me entendre. Fillis? no sé 💀

9:35 a. m. · 12 d'ag. de 2018

Figure 14 '*I have two daughters and a younger son. I can't say* els meus fills [generic masculine]*, I have the feeling of betraying the girls, who were there, and existed, before he was born. With* "elles" [generic feminine] *there's no problem, the boy accepts the* [generic] *feminine. But when I'm away from home, I duplicate the plural so that I can be understood.* Fillis [GNL]*? I don't know*'.

The link with other struggles for equality and social justice is also oftentimes made explicit:

A tota la gent que se'n fot del fet que les persones no binàries busquin fórmules lingüístiques per identificar-se, m'agradaria recordar-lis que fa cent anys hi havia gent que se'n fotia del fet que les dones volguessin votar.

12:16 a. m. · 20 de març de 2021

Figure 15 '*To all people who are making fun of the fact that non-binary people are looking for linguistic forms to identify with, I'd like to remind them that a hundred years ago there were people making fun of the fact that women wanted to vote*'.

In sum, some of our Twitter findings showed genuine interest, and even enthusiastic endorsements grounded on arguments of visibilisation, empowerment, and a sense of democratic agency in the linguistic realm, even if oftentimes ridden with hesitation.

Negative Attitudes

We have already mentioned that our search yielded significantly more examples of negative attitudes towards GNL than positive ones. Oftentimes the rejection was accompanied by condescending explanations repeating the traditional normative arguments in favour of the generic masculine, even going as far as claiming that it was GNL itself that was being exclusive:

"tots" és el gènere no marcat i, per tant, inclou tots els gèneres (masculí, femení, nobinari...). si et refereixes a "totis" tan sols estàs parlant a persones no binàries, i si ho fas serivr per a tothom les estàs invisibiltzant. és lingüística, potser no vas anar gaire a classe

10:11 p. m. · 14 de juny de 2022

Figure 16 'Tots [masculine] *is the unmarked gender, and so it includes all genders (masculine, feminine, non-binary . . .). With* "totis" *you're talking only to non-binary people, and if you use it to refer to everyone, then you're making them invisible. It's linguistics, maybe you didn't go much to class*'.

Rejecters expanded their arguments beyond resisting change due to lack of familiarity and disruption in their linguistic comfort. In fact, we found many examples of calling the use of GNL an imposition, mimicking current phobic ideas about the dangers that visibilising certain gender identities pose for more hegemonic ones:

Mira nen, tu te pots sentir i referirte a tu com vulguis.
Un altre tema es q obliguis a la resta de la població a referirnos com tu vulguis.
Aixo q demanes es el mateix q oligar a algú a parlar en l'idioma q tu vulguis.
Tirania i manca de llibertat d'expressió.
Nen es a posta.

11:08 a. m. · 20 de març de 2021

Figure 17 '*Look, dude, you can feel and refer to yourself however you want. Another issue is if you force the rest of the population to refer to you the way you want. What you're asking for is the same as forcing someone to speak the language you want. Tyranny and lack of freedom of speech. Dude is on purpose*'.

Furthermore, in spite of it being portrayed as a linguistic debate, a great deal of responses reflected attitudes that did not refer to GNL per se, but to those who use it, showing the politicisation of the issue. In some instances, we found tweets that were blatantly hostile to GNL, to the point of bordering not only on genderphobia (especially misogyny and transphobia), but also, for example, xenophobia:

Comença la selectivitat a l'Afganistàn! Molta sort a totis!

324.cat @324cat · 16 de juny de 2022
I la #324mésvistes Selectivitat 2022: tots els exàmens i correccions bit.ly/3NQO7t0

Figure 18 A Twitter user retweets news about college entrance exams in Catalonia. Presumably because of the student with a headscarf, they tweet: '*College entrance exams start in Afghanistan! Good luck to* totis!'

In some other instances, the dismissal was made somewhat more indirectly, for instance, linking GNL to a fake feminism or fake progressivist ideology (woke culture):

Això és feminisme, i no tota la merda aquesta de @taniaverge, d'ERC, @najat_driouech la CUP i les totis 🖐️

> **Patrycia Centeno** @PoliticayModa · 16 d'oct. de 2022
> La escaladora iraní Elnaz Rekabi compite por primera vez sin velo 🎗️ ✨
> #IranRevolution #powerdressing #MashaAmini

10:15 a. m. · 18 d'oct. de 2022

Figure 19 Retweet of a video with Iranian climber Elnaz Rebaki, who participated in international championships without a headscarf: '*This is feminism, not that bullshit by* [left political leaders] *and their* totis'.

Some arguments based their dismissal on the questioning of linguistic deterministic views, by claiming that GNL is an ineffective tool for social change:

Les societats amb llengües que no desdoblen, són més igualitàries? Tenim algun indici que fer això serveixi per res?

5:07 p. m. · 11 d'ag. de 2018

Figure 20 '*Are societies with languages that do not duplicate* [grammatical gender] *more egalitarian? Do we have any evidence that this is useful*?'

No m'importaria fer l'esforç si ha de servir per alguna cosa, però busco i no trobo estudis que demostrin que canviar el llenguatge canviï la societat. Tant de bo! Em convenç més gent con @CarmeJunyent

6:14 p. m. · 14 d'ag. de 2018

Figure 21 '*I wouldn't mind making the effort if it got anywhere, but I'm searching and I can't find studies proving that society changes by modifying the language. I wish! I'm more convinced by people like* [well-known anti-GNL linguist]'.

A more non-committal approach claims that the issue is untimely and it is taking attention away from more important endeavours:

En un futur espero no tenir aquesta conversa:
- Pare, mentre el feixisme i la ultradreta anava creixent, què feia l'esquerra?
- Discutir si deiem tots, totes o totis.

7:59 a. m. · 27 d'oct. de 2022

Figure 22 '*I hope I won't have this conversation in the future: – Dad, while fascism and the alt-right were growing, what were the leftists doing? – Discussing whether we should say* tots, totes *or* totis'.

This argument takes a very personal turn for the context of Catalonia:

"No molesti, estem treballant per tots, totes i totis."

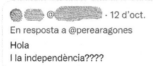
· 12 d'oct.
En resposta a @perearagones
Hola
I la independència????

1:49 p. m. · 13 d'oct. de 2022 des de Manresa, Espanya · Twitter for Android

Figure 23 As a tweet asks the current autonomous Catalan President about independence, another user answers: '*Do not disturb, we are working for* tots, totes, *and* totis'.

Estarem discutint si és totis, tots i totes, tot@s o totxs i quan sortim al
carrer, esgotats de no haver arribat a cap conclusió, ens diran molt
amablement que por favor en castellano

11:29 a. m. · 25 de jul. de 2021

Figure 24 '*We'll be discussing whether it's gonna be* tots, tots i totes, tot@s, *or*
totxs, *and then when we go out on the street, exhausted for not having concluded
anything, we'll be very politely told "please* [speak] *Spanish"*'.

Resorting to humour is abundant, and we are including it in the section of
negative responses, because oftentimes it takes the shape of mocking and ridiculing the neomorpheme, normally by simply substituting all vowels by < i >:

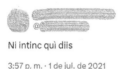

Ni intinc quì diis

3:57 p. m. · 1 de jul. de 2021

Figure 25 Ni intinc quì diis = No entenc què dius, '*I don't understand what
you're saying*'.

Again, oftentimes mocking went beyond the realm of the linguistic and
morphed into a wider genderphobic attack disguised as a joke:

A mi m'ofèn que us dirigiu al meu gènere no definit amb el llenguatge
parlat, no m'identifico, exigeixo que us comuniqueu amb mi xiulant
melodies de música.

5:02 p. m. · 20 de març de 2021

Figure 26 '*I'm offended by you referring to my non-defined gender with spoken
language, I don't identify with it, I demand that you communicate with me by
whistling musical melodies*'.

Back to serious language matters, some tweeters have the strong feeling that
the innovation goes against what Catalan should look like:

nomes es carregarse el llenguatge

10:10 p. m. · 14 de juny de 2022

Figure 27 '*It's just destroying the language*'.

A Few Points Specific to Catalan GNL

We mentioned before that Catalan poses its own challenges when it comes to the grammar of GNL; while those are certainly not unique, they also do not hold for all languages. The same can be said about arguments for or against GNL that refer specifically to the sociolinguistic situation of Catalan. For example, the acknowledgement of its perceived vulnerability, which is used to advocate a conservative approach:

La societat ha de ser inclusiva. El llenguatge és una tradició que ve de molts segles enrera. Pot evolucionar però canviar-lo massa el pot destruir ! Tampoc podem ser tots de compte vegetarians. Per molt que hi hagi bones raons jo i el meu cos volem seguir menjant carn !

3:58 p. m. · 1 de jul. de 2021

Figure 28 '*Society needs to be inclusive. Language is a tradition that goes back centuries. It can evolve but changing it too much can break it! We can't either suddenly all become vegetarians. Even if there are good reasons, I and my body want to keep eating meat!*'

Relatedly, Catalan GNL is dismissed on the basis of it being senseless, unauthorised, and illegitimate, and distorting/polluting the nature of Catalan, as already seen in Figure 7. The argument of GNL being an imposition is also brought close to home for Catalans, who keep in their collective memory the enduring effects of linguistic policies and hegemonic linguistic practices, as also seen in Figure 17.

On the positive side, a widespread cosmopolitan ideology celebrates an up-to-date Catalan language joining an international trend, in sharp contrast to an always present portrayal of linguistic minorities as clinging to the past:

Psalm per als construïts en Terres Salvatges, de Becky Chambers (
@MaiMesLlibres, trad. @annallis). El primer llibre amb llenguatge nobinari directe (elli) que llegeixo en català. Uni mongi i un robot es
descobreixen, ells i les seves societats

Figure 29 '*A Psalm for the Wild-Built, by Becky Chambers. [. . .] The first book in specifically non-binary language* (elli) *that I read. A cleric* [GNL] *and a robot discover each other, themselves and their societies.*'

Finally, the language endangerment narrative seen here is complemented by the ever-present threat of language shift. In the following tweet, a defendant of Catalan GNL eloquently snaps at the attacks, hitting where it hurts the most:

Llavors, les persones no binàries catalanes, que parlin en anglès. No?

9:28 a. m. · 21 de jul. de 2021

Figure 30 '*Then non-binary Catalan people should speak English, right?*'

Conclusion

The grammar of Catalan GNL has been coined, and (although still presenting some variation and a few morphological hesitations) it is being used in a stable enough way by those who wish to use it. A corpus-based study to find out how extensive its use really is would be pertinent (on the lines of Kalinowski, 2020, or the aforementioned Fundeu, 2020). As Kalinowski (2019) also points out, it is not quite clear whether at the moment the use of GNL could be considered a simple discursive strategy linked to political stances (also Gustafsson Sendén et al., 2015), or a true variety on its way to entering standard use. What it does mean is that the emergence of GNL in Catalan puts Catalan on the same page as the other languages around it, and this can be seen as a sign of its vitality.

Language users make linguistic choices that reflect their ideologies, which in turn depend on the assignment of social, moral, or political meanings associated with their languages (Woolard & Frekko, 2013). The phenomenon of GNL is far from being a purely linguistic one; rather, as Hornsby (2019a) points out, it can be classified as a sociological and cultural one: indeed GNL responds to a very real need to visibilise and enact certain gender groups and identities that have been systematically erased (Gal & Irvine, 1995) from the public sphere, and it is that, more than its linguistic unfamiliarity, what causes discomfort in certain spaces

(Sánchez & Mayo, 2019). Catalan society at large can be characterised by being a progressive and egalitarian community, as voting patterns, governmental gender-equality agencies, and medical approaches to gender-sensitive topics like trans-genderism, for example, show. It is thus surprising that the response to GNL is saliently one of clinging to the norm, rejection, and ridicule, to the extent that we can take Twitter as a measurement of it. Given the survival pressures on this minoritised language (with an unfriendly state and a weak local government adding to the intense contact with Spanish and English), it is possible that speakers who wish to signal their commitment to social equality through their linguistic practices might not trust Catalan to fulfil this function for long, and thus they find (yet another) reason to switch to another language within their linguistic repertoire (Pera-Ros, 2021; Olid, 2018). What this means for Catalan and other languages struggling to keep their relevance for the speakers they have left or for others to come, should be thought out very carefully.

Discussion: Queering Language Revitalisation

Holly Cashman

Introduction and Positionality

In recent years, researchers have begun to grapple with sexuality and gender identity and expression in research on multilingualism and language acquisition. This collection aims to build on that important work, stretching it in the direction of research on language revitalisation.

Too often, the language practices of LGBTQ+ speakers have been marginalised in research of language revitalisation, just as multilingualism has too often been ignored or pushed to the side in research on LGBTQ+ language practices. In this short section, I first ask what it means to queer multilingualism research, then explore what is normative in language revitalisation research. I continue on to pose several questions related to multilingualism, minoritised languages, language revitalisation, and sexuality that might be of use to researchers across a variety of contexts, and in doing so, I highlight the key contributions from the research published in this collection by John Walsh on Irish, Michael Hornsby on Breton, Eva J. Daussà and Renée Pera-Ros on Catalan, and Jonathan Morris and Samuel Parker on Welsh. I finish by describing what it means to adopt a queer lens in language revitalisation research, what queer methodologies might benefit language revitalisation research(ers), and how queering multilingualism may lead to a deeper understanding of language revitalisation efforts and activism. Finally, I conclude with thoughts about where a queered research programme in language revitalisation might lead.

I want to start by noting that my background related to this topic is in language maintenance and shift, and I am not at all well versed in the extensive language revitalisation literature. While the two areas are obviously interconnected, I am very much an outsider looking in and commenting, which has both advantages and disadvantages.

Queering Multilingualism?

What does it mean to queer a research agenda? While it is valuable to explore the language practices of people who have traditionally been left out of research in a given area (e.g. LGBTQ+ individuals and communities in language revitalisation research), doing that alone does not constitute queering a research agenda. Rather, to queer a research agenda involves investigating and interrogating what is normative, how those norms came to be and how they are maintained, perhaps taking up new methods, asking new questions, discarding or complicating received terminology, and engaging in new ways as scholars.

Milani and Levon (2017) approach queering multilingualism by 'investigat[ing] the intersections of mobility, sexuality and citizenship, and the role played by multilingualism and multi-semioticity in mediating such relationships'. They describe this queer multilingualism approach as 'a fresh, queer perspective on the growing scholarship on language and citizenship', arguing that 'a tight analytical focus on multilingualism and multi-semioticity' can contribute to the study of queer migration and to the study of citizenship and the politics of belonging (Milani & Levon, 2017: 529). Similarly, I have advocated for 'queering bilingualism' (Cashman, 2018), which involved centring the experiences of queer Mexican and Latinx individuals and communities as well as engaging with an attempt to make visible the impact that forces of heteronormativity and racial hegemony exercise not only on these individuals and communities but on *our research of* the multilingual language practices they employ. Also key to the approach I took to queering bilingualism/multilingualism is a focus on *languaging* rather than *languages*.

In other words, we have to start by questioning the assumptions and deeply held beliefs in the field; in this next part I hope to contribute to this effort by flagging what some of the norms involved in research on language revitalisation might be, although I leave it to those more deeply rooted in the research area to pursue this further.

What is Normative in Language Revitalisation Research?

Fishman's (1991) *Reversing Language Shift* was ground breaking in its call for a shift in focus from documenting language shift and death to studying the practices that support language maintenance and reverse language shift. This approach focuses its attention squarely on the heteronormative family unit, on promoting the intergenerational transmission of the 'mother tongue'. In many ways, Fishman is still the blueprint. Journalist James Griffiths (2021) in his recently published popular book about language revitalisation summarises: 'decades of work in language revitalization has provided a clear model for minority tongues around the world. Work begins at home, encouraging and supporting parents to use their native languages, and in pre-schools, with immersion kindergartens' (Griffiths, 2021: 190). Leanne Hinton (2013) writes: 'many of us would say that the most important locus of language revitalization is not in the schools, but rather the home, the last bastion from which the language was lost, and the primary place where first language acquisition occurs. Those who dream of language revitalization ultimately desire the natural transmission of the language from parent to child' (Hinton, 2013: xiv).

In addition to the focus on the heteronormative family unit and intergenerational transmission, what are other concepts in language revitalisation that merit critique? Questioning the binary concepts of 'native speaker' and 'non-native speaker' led to the new and useful concept of 'new speaker' (O'Rourke, 2018) and further theorising of 'speakerness' (Pujolar & O'Rourke, 2022). We could ask what concepts like 'mother tongue', like 'prestige', 'support', 'vitality', 'authenticity' and 'visibility', like 'in group' and 'out group' members bring to the table in terms of assumptions about language practices, about communities, and about speakers. (These are only terms pulled out of a hat; this is not intended as a comprehensive list or even a list of terms most relevant or most in need of interrogating.) We need to ask what they contribute but also what they might keep us from seeing, understanding? We can use terms like 'new speaker', minority/minoritised language, or 'X-speaking community' as a shorthand, and yet we must always remember to problematise these terms, trouble their conventional understandings, expose the messiness that they tend to tidy up or paper over. We must remember to view notions such as 'authenticity' or 'status' as a process, something accomplished in interaction rather than an objective, static reality.

Inspired by the sections by Hornsby and Walsh in this Element, I wonder when we focus on institutional support and the legal status of languages, what are we not focussing on? How can we question the idea that those interested in language revitalisation are looking inward and backward rather than reaching outward and forward, particularly as we think about topics like gender inclusive language? What assumptions do we make about the role of experts and policymakers vis-à-vis community members, artists, and writers versus teachers?

And, of course, also looking at the people we do and do not include in our research is part of this. How can we widen our scope to include individuals, families, and communities outside of the heteronormative family unit in our approach to language revitalisation? How can we examine language revitalisation while resisting heteronormativity (and homonormativity)? Wright's (2020) work on 'critical kinship' and language socialisation in queer families is one direction; another is Rowlett's (2020) work on queer language socialisation and looking at queer people without children. What would it mean to decentre the hypothetical future child (Edelman, 2004) in language revitalisation research? Like the political discourse Edelman critiqued, language revitalisation discourse has also centred on transmission of the endangered language to a (hypothetical, future) child. Would we be able to conceive of a language revitalisation effort without the figure of the child and what Edelman called 'the Ponzi scheme of reproductive futurism' (Edelman, 2004: p. 4)?

Key Contributions from This Element

The sections in this Element are rich and compelling investigations of queer speakers of minoritised languages and attempts to make minoritised languages more inclusive. They each bring an openness and fresh perspective to how individuals, including LGBTQ+ speakers, and communities are orienting to language modernisation and revitalisation efforts. Each of these sections makes key contributions and shares valuable insights for the project of queering language revitalisation.

John Walsh's section takes an in-depth look at what queer(ed) language revitalisation efforts might look like, from a queer take on the Irish-language conversation circle to an immersive exhibit at the Dublin Fringe Festival by a queer, Irish-speaking artists collective called AerachAiteachGaelach ('gay, queer, Irish-speaking'). He pushes back against the notion that Irish is a language 'unsuited for the modern, urbanised world' and the 'perceived link between the language and conservatism'. In the case of Alan Walpole, whose life story is the subject of the immersive exhibit, he explores how becoming a new speaker of Irish and coming out as a gay man might be parallel and even intertwined trajectories. In Walsh's section we see an example of how queer *community* (Queercal Comhrá, AerachAiteachGaelach), not the heteronormative family, is the locus of language revitalisation. We also see how migration rather than integration within a close-knit in-group of minoritised language speakers prompts one individual's efforts to reconnect with Irish. Walsh's case also dramatically drives home the ways that family can be hostile to queer youth (and adults), making the home a painful and contested space rather than a site of warmth and intergenerational language transmission, even if the minoritised language were the home language, which was not the case for Alan Walpole. In Walsh's section, we see a completely different take on intergenerational transmission. Rather than the language passing from parent to child, Walsh conveys the intergenerational transmission of queer history and queer stories through a new speaker's telling and an artists' collective's imagining and creatively exhibiting a coming out and coming 'home' experience of an older gay man to younger members of the queer, Irish-speaking community.

Jonathan Morris and Samuel Parker's section looks at how LGBTQ+ speakers of Welsh position themselves in terms of their Welsh-speaking identities and queer identities, whether they see any intersection, and what barriers LGBTQ+ speakers of Welsh might find in achieving full cohesion between their Welsh-speaking and queer identities. They identify several sub-themes that emerge from their interviewees' reflections on their Welsh and LGBTQ+ identities: tradition and rurality, English as the language of the LGBTQ+ community, and representation. In Morris and Parker, we see that not all LGBTQ+ Welsh speakers see a conflict between their Welsh-speaking and queer identities (in contrast to the 'split' described by Alan in Walsh's section), although many do. We must not assume a priori that there is a split or a conflict and go from there in our research, when doing so may erase or ignore a position that speakers in the community hold toward their minoritised language and gender and/or sexuality. Morris and Parker look at intersecting identities but not necessarily intersectionality. They bring in questions of age/generation, mobility, and rural/urban identities, ideological links speakers draw on in their positioning. Like the queer conversation circle in the Irish community described by Walsh, Morris, and Parker also see a queering of Welsh cultural traditions, such as one participant's analysis of the campness of the Eisteddfod festival. Both Walsh and Morris and Parker touch on the emotional and affective aspects of speaking minoritised languages and the connection between queer feelings/feeling queer (which brings to my mind Muñoz 2009).

Eva J. Daussà and Renée Pera-Ros examine the attitudes of Catalan speakers towards neo-morphemes and neo-pronouns in Catalan in data from the social media landscape, identifying themes in Twitter (now called X) discourse ranging from authority and legitimacy to linguistic agency. While Catalan boasts an enviable ten million speakers, it is seen as threatened by low rates of social use and by hostile political campaigns against its use in institutional spaces or as a requirement for certain types of employment. Daussà and Pera-Ros explore how Catalan Twitter users respond both positively and negatively to neo-morphemes and neo-pronouns in the language. Rather than assume the value of institutional support or take for granted the authority of certain institutions, this research demonstrates how the authority to decide what is and is not acceptable in a language is established and contested through interaction, including social media discourse. Likewise, for language users the legitimacy of new forms and speakers' agency are negotiated and the value of modernisation and inclusion of LGBTQ+ speakers in the vitality of a minoritised or endangered language is a matter of debate, as speakers align their language choices with their ideologies. Importantly, in exploring the negative reactions to inclusive language, Daussà and Pera-Ros help to elucidate some of the ways that language revitalisation may make use of homophobic and genderphobic discourse.

Lastly, Michael Hornsby's section looks at the ways a Breton-speaking community is making Breton more gender inclusive and more LGBTQ+ affirming, particularly focussing on the creation and publication of a trilingual (Breton-French-English) inclusive lexicon by a feminist organisation. Like Daussà and Pera-Ros, Hornsby's work questions the traditional wisdom that modernisation is at odds with language maintenance and that authenticity rather than inclusion is a key to vitality. Hornsby uses examples drawn from a variety of sources to not only describe some of the strategies used to innovate in Breton but to resist innovation. In sum, we are invited to consider how the resistance of notions of language purity and the practice of modernising strategies or language innovation may open up the possibility of queer speakers to use minoritised languages in their daily life and their political activism and thus positively impact a language's vitality.

Adopting a Queer Lens in Language Revitalisation Research

By way of conclusion, I will reiterate that I contend that a queer language revitalisation needs to be involved in not only making the lives and experiences and language practices of LGBTQ+ speakers of minoritised languages visible and legible and lifting up the ways that gender inclusive and LGBTQ+ affirming language can help broaden the notion of to whom minoritised languages belong and who belongs in minoritised language communities, but also in exposing the heteronormativity of language revitalisation. This will no doubt involve uncovering the assumptions that the terminology we use makes and making visible how research in language revitalisation may be tied up in and compromised by patriarchal and conservative ideologies. It will involve exploring the heterogeneity within the 'in-group' of minoritised language speaking communities and exploring how forces like migration, contact, technology, innovation, and change can support as well as undermine language revitalisation. Queer(ed) language revitalisation research will need to explore how LGBTQ+ (new) speakers articulate their identities intersubjectively outside the interview context, how they position themselves, and what the consequences are for the understanding (their own and others') of their belonging and also how understandings of gender and sexuality are at work in the language practices of non-LGBTQ+ speakers.

In short, I have three main suggestions for queering language revitalisation:

(1) Look at queering methodologies (e.g. Milani & Borba, 2022; Ghaziani & Brim, 2019) to explore how we might ask different questions, apply different lenses, and push the field forward. This will not only involve

studying what LGBTQ+ speakers of minoritised languages are doing and thinking and feeling but will also involve studying and exposing homophobic discourses within language revitalisation efforts. We need to refuse to limit ourselves to what has been done before and how it has been done. We must allow ourselves to be surprised, to use scavenger methods (Plummer, 2005; Hennen, 2008), to refuse to be limited by disciplinary norms, and to collect data queerly, and analyse data queerly. This is not just about research methods, but the entire process – we also need to find ways to write, edit, and review scholarship queerly, to conference queerly; in this I am inspired by Bill Leap's reflections on Lavender Languages Studies or what a Lavender Languages Project looks like (Marzullo & Leap, 2022).

(2) Consider how we engage as collaborators in the work that is being done. In this regard I was really moved by and inspired by the impact that the flyer in the window of an Irish-language club advertising a Queer conversation circle (Queercal Comhrá) had on Alan, as described in Walsh's section, as well as Hornsby's work on the feminist collective's inclusive lexicon. In his concept of 'allied linguistics', Borba (2022) argues that we must engage as collaborators, as allies in the work of queer, trans, and non-binary people who are asserting their identities in the public sphere to combat invisibility and demanding inclusion. What kinds of 'radically empathic' and 'activism-informed research' could an 'allied' language revitalisation research take on in the urgency of endangered, minoritised languages? And how can we do this while also being allies in feminist, queer, anti-racist activism, resisting nationalist and populist discourses that often accompany language revitalisation efforts? How does this depend on who we are in relation to the community? Borba writes that applied linguistics 'has much to gain from seriously (and critically) engaging allyship as a methodological heuristic to foster social justice' and he encourages us to 'unpack the role of language in establishing, perpetuating, and disrupting oppressive institutional regimes and practices'. What could be gained in language revitalisation research by bringing to bear the concepts of *poder* and *potencia* (Hall, Borba & Hiramoto 2021), informed by Argentine activist and thinker Verónica Gago (2020). *Poder* (power) is top-down, institutionalised, and maintains the status quo, while *potencia* (potency) is bottom-up, dynamic, and driving change; *potencia* can open up new directions, uncover the language of *poder* by 'deployment of counter-power' (Gago, 2020: 2).

(3) Finally, have hope. Drawing on Martínez (2009), who argued for a 'sociolinguistics of hope' in research on Spanish language maintenance in the US, Hiramoto, Borba, and Hall (2020) and Muñoz's (2009) concept of queer futurity, look beyond what is to that which could and should be.

References

Abalain, H., 1989. *Destin des langues celtiques*. Paris: Ophrys.

Abbou, J., 2011. 'Double gender marking in French: A linguistic practice of antisexism'. *Current Issues in Language Planning* 12 (1), 55–75.

Académie francaise, 2017. 'Déclaration de l'Académie française sur l'écriture dite "inclusive"'. Déclaration de l'Académie française sur l'écriture dite 'inclusive'. https://bit.ly/4cy3x11 (accessed 15 April 2023).

Amarelo, D., 2019. 'A (de)construción identitaria homosexual na conversa: Implicacións socioculturais no discurso gay galego'. *Madrygal: Revista de Estudios Gallegos* 22, 31–49.

Angouri, J., 2021. 'Language, gender, and sexuality: Sketching out the field'. In Angouri, J. and Baxter, J. (eds.), *The Routledge Handbook of Language, Gender, and Sexuality*. London: Routledge, 1–22.

Ansara, Y. G. and Hegarty, P., 2014. 'Methodologies of misgendering: Recommendations for reducing cisgenderism in psychological research'. *Feminist Psychology* 24, 259–270.

Ar Rouz, D., 2016. 'À la poursuite du diamant glaz: Le standard breton'. *Sociolinguistica* 30 (1), 145–174.

Bailey, A., 2019. '"Girl-on-girl culture": Constructing normative identities in a corpus of sex advice for queer women'. *Journal of Language and Sexuality* 8 (2), 195–220.

BBC, 2022a. *Oes cynrychiolaeth LHDTC+ ddigonol yn y sîn gerddoriaeth Gymraeg?* [Is there enough LGBTQ+ representation in the Welsh-language music scene?]. www.bbc.co.uk/cymrufyw/60290333 (accessed 18 January 2023).

BBC, 2022b. *'Dal ffordd i fynd' i fod yn gynhwysol at bobl LHDTC+* [Still a way to go to be inclusive towards LGBTQ+ people]. www.bbc.co.uk/cymrufyw/62418244 (accessed 18 January 2023).

BBC, 2023a. *Siaradwyr Cymraeg anneuaidd eisiau iaith LHDTC+ gynhwysol* [Non-binary Welsh speakers want inclusive LGBTQ+ language]. www.bbc.co.uk/cymrufyw/64166667 (accessed 18 January 2023).

BBC, 2023b. *Sefydlu Eisteddfod leol ar gyfer pobl LHDTC+?* [Establish a local Eisteddfid for LGBTQ+ people?]. www.bbc.co.uk/cymrufyw/64240610 (accessed 18 January 2023).

Berger, M., 2019. 'A guide to how gender-neutral language is developing in the world'. *The Guardian*. https://wapo.st/3VRWzyA (accessed 15 April 2023).

Boellstorff, T. and Leap, W. L., 2004. 'Introduction: Globalization and "new" articulations of same-sex desire'. In Leap, W. L. and Boellstorff, T. (eds.), *Speaking in Queer Tongues: Globalization and Gay Language*. Urbana: University of Illinois Press, 1–22.

Bonnin, J. E. and Coronel, A. A., 2021. 'Attitudes toward gender-neutral Spanish: Acceptability and adoptability'. *Frontiers in Sociology* 6, 616–629.

Borba, R., (ed.), 2020. *Discursos transviados: Por uma linguística queer*. São Paulo: Cortez Editora.

Borba, R., 2022. 'Animating other wor(l)ds: Transformations of language and social justice (Notes on "allied linguistics")'. American Association of Applied Linguistics (AAAL). Pittsburgh, March 19–22.

Boroditsky, L., Schmidt, L. A., and Phillips, W., 2003. 'Sex, syntax, and semantics'. In: Getner, D. and Goldin-Meadow, S. (eds.) *Language in mind: advances in the study of language and thought*. Cambridge: MIT Press, 61–79.

Boudreau, A., 2016. À l'ombre de la langue légitime: L'Acadie dans la Francophonie. Paris: Classiques Garnier.

Boudreau, A. and Dubois, L., 2005. 'L'affichage a Moncton: Miroir ou masque?' *Revue de l'Universite de Moncton* 36 (1), 185–217. https://doi .org/10.7202/011993ar.

Braun V., and Clarke V., 2006. 'Using thematic analysis in psychology'. *Qualitative Resesarch in Psychology* 3 (2), 77–101.

Braun, V. and Clarke, V., 2022. *Reflexive Thematic Analysis: A Practical Guide*. London: Sage.

Braun, V. and Clarke, V., 2023. 'Toward good practice in thematic analysis: Avoiding common problems and be(com)ing a knowing researcher'. *International Journal of Transgender Health* 24 (1), 1–6.

Broudic, F., 2009. *Parler breton au XXIe siècle: Le nouveau sondage de TMO-Régions*. Brest: Emgleo Breiz.

Brutt-Griffler, J., and Kim, S., 2017. 'In their own voices: Development of English as a gender-neutral language'. *English Today* 34 (1), 12–19.

Burke, P. J. and Stryker, S., 2016. 'Identity theory: Progress in relating the two strands'. In Stets, J. E. and Serpe, R. T. (eds.), *New Directions in Identity Theory and Research*. Oxford: Oxford University Press, 657–692.

Butler, J., 1990. *Gender Trouble: Feminism and the Subversion of Identity*. Abingdon: Routledge.

Caldwell, S., 2018. 'Marxism, feminism and trangender politics'. *International Socialism* 157, 25–52.

Carlin, P. and Mac Giolla Chríost, D., 2016. 'A standard for language? Policy, territory, and constitutionality in a devolving Wales'. In Durham, M. and Morris, J. (eds.), *Sociolinguistics in Wales*. London: Palgrave Macmillan, 93–119.

Cashman, H., 2018. *Queer, Latinx, and Bilingual: Narrative Resources in the Negotiation of Identities*. Abingdon: Routledge.

Castillo Sánchez, S. and Mayo, S., 2019. 'El language inclusivo como "norma" de empatía e identidad: Reflexiones entre docentes y futures profesores'. *Literatura y lingüística* (40), 377–391.

Central Statistics Office, 2017. *Census of Population 2016. Profile 10: Education, Skills and the Irish Language*. Cork: Central Statistics Office. www.cso.ie/en/releasesandpublications/ep/p-cp10esil/p10esil/.

Central Statistics Office, 2022. *Census of Population 2022. Profile 8: The Irish Language and Education*. Cork: Central Statistics Office. https://bit.ly/3VLk9Nx.

Chantreau, K. and Moal, S., 2022. 'The transmission of Breton in the family: The effect of family rupture and recomposition'. In Hornsby, M., McLeod, W. (eds), *Transmitting Minority Languages: Complementary Reversing Language Shift Strategies*. Palgrave Studies in Minority Languages and Communities. Cham: Palgrave Macmillan, 247–275.

Clarke V. and Braun V., 2017. 'Thematic analysis'. *Journal of Positive Psychology* 12 (3), 297–298.

Coady, A., 2018. 'The origin of sexism in language'. *Gender and Language* 12 (3), 271–293.

Del Valle, J., 2018. 'La política de la incomodidad. Notas sobre gramática y lenguaje inclusivo'. *Anuario de Glotopolítica* (August 28th).

Cor, D. N. and Chan, C. D., 2017. 'Intersectional feminism and LGBTIQQA+ psychology: Understanding our present by exploring our past'. In Ruth, R. and Santacruz, E. (eds.), *LGBT Psychology and Mental Health: Emerging Research and Advances*. Santa Barbara: Praeger, 109–132.

Crenshaw, K., 1989. 'Demarginalizing the intersection of race and sex: A black feminist critique of antidiscrimination doctrine, feminist theory and anti-racist politics'. *University of Chicago Legal Forum* 1989 (1), Article 8. https://bit.ly/4c9fvic (accessed 18 January 2023).

Deuchar, M., Donnelly, K. and Piercy, C., 2016. '"Mae pobl monolingual yn minority": Factors favouring the production of code switching by Welsh–English bilingual speakers'. In Durham, M. and Morris, J. (eds.), *Sociolinguistics in Wales*. London: Palgrave Macmillan, 209–239.

Dołowy-Rybińska, N., 2020. 'Informal bilingual teachers' language practices and the consequences on pupils' language choices in a situation of unequal bilingualism: The case of an Upper Sorbian education system'. *Multilingua: Journal of Cross-Cultural and Interlanguage Communication* 39 (2), 169–191.

Dołowy-Rybińska, N., 2022. 'Native and non-native speakers' school language practices and transmission in Upper Lusatia'. In Hornsby, M. and McLeod, W. (eds.), *Transmitting Minority Languages: Complementary Reversing Language Shift Strategies*. Cham: Springer, 139–164.

Doty, A., 1993. *Making Things Perfectly Queer: Interpreting Mass Culture*. Duluth: University of Minnesota Press.

Driscoll-Evans, P. R., 2020. Sexual citizenship beyond the metropolis: Bareback sex, chemsex and loneliness in a rural county in the United Kingdom. PhD thesis, University of Essex. https://bit.ly/3VuoR0R (accessed 12 February 2024).

Edelman, L., 2004. *No Future: Queer Theory and the Death Drive*. Durham: Duke University Press.

Everett, C. 2011. 'Gender, pronouns, and thought: The ligature between epicene pronouns and a more neutral gender perception'. *Gender and Language* 5 (1), 133–152.

Fishman, J., 1991. *Reversing Language Shift: Theoretical and Empirical Foundations of Assistance to Threatened Languages*. Clevedon: Multilingual Matters.

Fuertes Gutiérrez, M., 2022. 'Lenguaje inclusivo y universidad: Guías para el lenguaje no sexista'. Online presentation at the *Seminario ELEUK*, October 14.

Fundeu (Instituto de Ingeniería del Conocimiento), 2020. 'Uso en Twitter de la x, la e y la @ para evitar la mención expresa del género'. https://fundeu.es/documentos/marcasinclusivastwitter.pdf (accessed 15 April 2023).

Gago, V., 2020. *Feminist International: How to Change Everything*. New York: Verso.

Gal, S., and Irvine, S. T., 1995. 'The boundaries of languages and disciplines: How ideologies construct difference'. *Social Research* 62 (4), 967–1001.

Geffard, V. 2022. 'Elles créent un lexique en breton du vocabulaire féministe qui englobe la communauté LGBTQIA+'. *Ouest France, Rennes*, 3 November. https://bit.ly/3VxlpCn (accessed: 8 June 2023).

Ghaziani, A. and Brim, M., 2019. 'Four provocations for an emerging field'. In Ghaziani, A. and M. Brim (eds.). *Imagining Queer Methods*. New York: New York University Press, 3–27.

Grieser, J., 2021. 'Critical race theory and the new sociolinguistics'. In Burkette, A. and Warhol, T. (eds.). *Crossing Borders, Making Connections: Interdisciplinarity in Linguistics*. Berlin: De Gruyter Mouton, 41–58.

Griffiths, J., 2021. *Speak Not: Empire, Identity and the Politics of Language.* London: Bloomsbury.

Gustafsson Sendén, M., Bäck, E. A. and Lindqvist, A., 2015. 'Introducing a gender-neutral pronoun in a natural gender language: The influence of time on attitudes and behavior'. *Frontiers in Psychology* 6 (893).

Gygax, P. and Gesto, N., 2007. 'Féminisation et lourdeur de texte'. *L'Année Psychologique* 107 (2), 239–255.

Hall, K., Borba, R. and Hiramoto, M., 2021. 'Relocating power: The feminist potency of language, gender and sexuality research'. *Gender and Language* 15 (1), 1–10.

Heller, M., 2001. 'Gender and public space in a bilingual school'. In Pavlenko, A., Blackledge, A., Piller, I. and Teutsch-Dwyer, M. (eds.). *Multilingualism, Second Language Learning and Gender.* Berlin: Mouton de Gruyter, 257–282.

Heller, M., 2006. *Linguistic Minorities and Modernity.* London: Continuum.

Heller, M., 2007. 'Bilingualism as ideology and practice'. In Heller, M. (ed.), *Bilingualism: A Social Approach.* London: Palgrave Macmillan, 1–22.

Heller, M. and Labrie, N., (eds.), 2003. *Discours et Identités: La Francité Canadienne entre Modernité et Mondialisation.* Fernelmont: Éditions Modulaires Européennes.

Hennen, P., 2008. *Faeries, Bears, and Leathermen: Men in the Community Queering the Masculine.* Chicago: University of Chicago Press.

Hinton, L., 2013. 'Introduction'. In Hinton, L. (ed.). *Bringing Our Languages Home: Language Revitalization for Families.* Berkeley: Heyday, xi–xx.

Hiramoto, M., Borba, R. and Hall, K., 2020. 'Hope in a time of crisis'. *Gender and Language* 14 (4), 347–357.

Hornsby, M., 2015. 'The "new" and "traditional" speaker dichotomy: Bridging the gap'. *International Journal of the Sociology of Language* 231 (1), 107–25.

Hornsby, M., 2017. 'Finding an ideological niche for new speakers in a minoritised language community'. *Language, Culture and Curriculum* 30 (1), 91–104.

Hornsby, M., 2019a. 'Gender-fair language in a minority setting: The case of Breton'. *Studia Celtica Posnaniensia* 4 (1), 59–74.

Hornsby, M., 2019b. 'Positions and stances in the hierarchization of Breton speakerhood'. *Journal of Multilingual and Multicultural Development* 40 (5), 392–403.

Hornsby, M. and McLeod, W. (eds.), 2022. *Transmitting Minority Languages: Complementary Reversing Language Shift Strategies.* Cham: Springer.

Hornsby, M., and Quentel, G., 2013. 'Contested varieties and competing authenticities: Neologisms in revitalised Breton'. *International Journal of the Sociology of Language* 223, 71–86.

Hornsby, M. and Vigers, D., 2018. '"New" speakers in the heartlands: Struggles for speaker legitimacy in Wales'. *Journal of Multilingual and Multicultural Development* 39 (5), 419–430.

James, D., 2010. *Llwyth* [Tribe]. Cardiff: Sherman Cymru.

Jaspal, R. and Bayley, J., 2020. *HIV and Gay Men: Clinical, Social and Psychological Aspects*. London: Palgrave Macmillan.

Jones, R., 2019. 'Place and identity: Wales, "Welshness" and the Welsh language'. *Geography* 104 (1), 19–27.

IEC, 2023. Minutes of the Plenary Session of October 20th. *Secció Filològica de l'Institut d'Estudis Catalans*.

Imborek, K. L., Nisly, N. L., Hesseltine, M. J., Grienke, J., Zikmund, T. A., Dreyer, N. R., et al., 2017. 'Preferred names, preferred pronouns, and gender identity in the electronic medical record and laboratory information system: is pathology ready?' *Journal of Pathologics Informatics* 8 (8), 42.

Kalinowski, S., 2019. 'Lenguaje inclusivo: Cambio lingüístico o cambio social'. *Revista CTBCBA* 141, 53–55.

Kalinowski, S., 2020. 'Lenguaje inclusivo en usuarios de Twitter en Argentina: Un estudio de corpus'. *Cuarenta Naipes* 2 (3), 233–259.

Katsiveli-Siachou, S., 2021. Intersections of sexuality and Greek national belonging: A conversation analytic approach. PhD thesis, Queen Mary, University of London.

Kaufmann, C. and Bohner, G., 2014. 'Masculine generics and gender-aware alternatives in Spanish'. *IZGOnZeit: Onlinezeitschrift des Interdisziplinären Zentrums für Geschlechterforschung (IZG)*, 8–17.

Kennard, H., 2022. 'Transmission of Breton among immersion-school students: The impact of home language'. In Hornsby, M., McLeod, W. (eds) *Transmitting Minority Languages: Complementary Reversing Language Shift Strategies*. Palgrave Studies in Minority Languages and Communities. Palgrave Macmillan, Cham, 247–278.

Kiger, M. E., and Varpio, L., 2020. 'Thematic analysis of qualitative data: AMEE Guide No. 131'. *Medical Teacher* 42 (8), 846–854.

Kircher, R., 2022. 'Intergenerational language transmission in Quebec: Patterns and predictors in the light of provincial language planning'. *International Journal of Bilingual Education and Bilingualism* 25 (2), 418–435.

Koch, M., 2008. *Language and Gender Research from a Queer Linguistic Perspective: A Critical Evaluation*. Saarbrücken: VDM, Verlag Dr Muller.

Lakoff, R.T., 1973. 'Language and woman's place'. *Language in Society* 2, 45–80.

——— 2021. *Fractures: Le féminisme et le mouvement LGBT en danger.* Joinville-le-Pont: Éditions Double Ponctuation.

Mac Eoghain, T., 2022. *An Foclóir Aiteach* (2nd ed.). Dublin: Union of Students in Ireland.

Maegusuku-Hewett, T., Raithby, M. and Willis, P., 2015. 'Life in the Pink Dragon's Den: Mental health services and social inclusion for LGBT people in Wales'. In Fish, J. and Karban, K. (eds.), *Lesbian, Gay, Bisexual and Trans Health Inequalities: International Perspectives in Social Work.* Bristol: Policy Press, 79–95.

Márquez Reiter, R. and Martín Rojo, M. (eds.), 2019. 'Special issue. Experiences of speakerhood: Migrant speakers' battles for inclusion in traditionally monolingual and bilingual contexts'. *International Journal of the Sociology of Language*, 257.

Martínez, G. A., 2009. 'Towards a sociolinguistics of hope: The inter-generational maintenance of Spanish and development of Spanish-speaking communities in the southwestern United States'. *Spanish in Context* 6 (1), 127–137.

Marzullo, M. and Leap, W., 2022. 'Where lavender languages and critical sexuality studies meet: Looking back, looking forward'. Roundtable discussion at Lavender Languages 28, Università di Catania, Catania, Italy, May 23.

McEvoy, E. and Ní É, C., 2021. 'Idir Mise agus Craiceann do Chluaise – script'. Copy with kind permission of Eoin McEvoy.

McEvoy, E. and Ní É, C., 2022. Interview with John Walsh, Galway, 8 April.

McEwan-Fujita, E., 2020. 'Gaelic revitalization efforts in Nova Scotia: Reversing language shift (RLS) in the 21st century'. In McEwan-Fujita, E. (ed.) *Gaelic Language Revitalization: Concepts and Challenges.* Halifax: Bradan Press, 287–314.

Milani, T. M., 2013. 'Are "queers" really "queer"? Language identity and same-sex desire in a South African online community'. *Discourse and Society* 24 (5), 615–633.

Milani, T. M. and Borba, R., 2022. 'Queer(ing) methodologies'. In Flick, U. (ed.), *The SAGE Handbook of Qualitative Research Design.* Thousand Oaks: Sage, 194–209.

Milani, T. M. and Levon, E., 2017. 'Queering multilingualism and politics: Regimes of mobility, citizenship and (in)visibility'. In Wodak, R. and Forchtner, B. (eds.), *The Routledge Handbook of Language and Politics.* Abingdon, Oxon: Routledge, 528–540.

Milroy, J., 2001. 'Language ideologies and the consequences of standardization'. *Journal of Sociolinguistics* 5 (4), 530–555.

Moretti, J., 2018. 'La RAE y el rechazo al lenguaje inclusivo'. *Letras* 7, 25–31.

Motschenbacher, H., 2011. 'Taking queer linguistics further: sociolinguistics and critical heteronormativity research'. *International Journal of the Sociology of Language*, 212, 149–179.

Moyano, J., (coord.), 2023. *Guia gramatical del llenguatge no binari*. Barcelona: Raig Verd.

Muñoz, J. E., 2009. *Cruising Utopia: The Then and There of Queer Futurity*. New York: NYU Press.

Murphy, J. and Mac Murchaidh, C., 2023. 'Fearann nua focal'. *Comhar* 83 (6), 38–40.

National Eisteddfod of Wales, 2022. Mas ar y Maes [Out on the Field]. https://bit.ly/4ca2O6C (accessed 18 January 2023).

Ní É, C. and McEvoy, E., 2021. 'Spotsholas ar thogra: AerachAiteachGaelach. Ciara Ní É agus Eoin McEvoy i mbun allagair le Róisín Ní Ghairbhí'. In Ní Mhuircheartaigh, É., Ní Ghairbhí, R. and Ó Liatháin, P. (eds), *Ó Chleamairí go Ceamaraí: Drámaíocht agus Taibhealaíona na Gaeilge faoi chaibidil*. Dublin: Cló Léann na Gaeilge, 259–272.

Nieves, G. P., and Hernández, D. I. S., 2022. 'El uso del lenguaje inclusivo en el habla de docentes y alumnos universitarios'. *Enletawa Journal* 15 (2), 1–34.

Northern Ireland Statistics and Research Agency, 2022a. *Census 2021: Main statistics for Northern Ireland. Statistical bulletin: Language.* 22 September 2022. Belfast: Northern Ireland Statistics and Research Agency. https://bit.ly/3z7dwvU.

Northern Ireland Statistics and Research Agency, 2022b. MS-B07: 'Frequency of speaking Irish' (Excel table). Belfast: Northern Ireland Statistics and Research Agency. www.nisra.gov.uk/publications/census-2021-main-statistics-language-tables.

Nossem, E., 2017. 'Queering lexicography: Balancing power relations in dictionaries'. In Baer, B. J. and Kaindl, K. (eds.), *Queering Translation, Translating the Queer: Theory, Practice, Activism*. New York: Routledge, 172–187.

Ó Tuathaigh, G., 2011. 'An stat, an fhéiniúlacht náisiúnta agus an teanga: Cás na hÉireann'. In Mac Cormaic, B. (ed.), *Féiniúlacht, Cultúr agus Teanga i Ré an Domhandaithe*. Dublin: Coiscéim, 76–112.

Ofis publik ar Brezhoneg, 2022. *Les chiffres de la rentrée scolaire de l'enseignement bilingue en 2022*. www.fr.brezhoneg.bzh/include/viewFile.php?idtf=4658&path=af%2F4658_983_Sifrou-DS-ar-c-helenn-divyezhek-2022_glg.pdf (accessed 17 April 2023).

Olid, B. 2018. Amb 'i' d'inclusiva. *Jornada*. 13 Agost 2018. http://catalallengua .blogspot.com/2018/08/amb-i-dinclusiva.html (accessed 15 April 2023).

O'Rourke, B., 2018. 'New speakers of minority languages'. In Hinton, L., Huss, L. and Roche, G. (eds.), *The Routledge Handbook of Language Revitalization*. New York: Routledge, 265–274.

O'Rourke, B. and Walsh, J., 2020. *New Speakers of Irish in the Global Context: New Revival?* London: Routledge.

O'Rourke, B., Pujolar, J. and Ramallo, F., 2015. 'New speakers of minority languages: The challenging opportunity – Foreword'. *International Journal of the Sociology of Language*, 231, 1–20.

Palys, T., 2008. 'Purposive sampling'. In Given, L. M. (ed.), *The Sage Encyclopedia of Qualitative Research Methods* (vol. 2). Los Angeles: Sage, 697–698.

Parra, M. L. and Serafini, E. J., 2021. '"Bienvenidxs todes": El lenguaje inclusivo desde una perspectiva crítica para las clases de español'. *Journal of Spanish Language Teaching* 8 (2), 143–160.

Penelope, J., 1988. 'Prescribed passivity: The language of sexism'. In the Nebraska Sociological Feminist Collective (eds.), *A Feminist Ethic for Social Science Research*. Lewiston/Queenston: Edwin Mellen Press, 119–138.

Pennycook, A., 2017. 'Language policy and local practices'. In García, O., Flores, N. and Spotti, M. (eds), *The Oxford Handbook of Language and Society*. Oxford: Oxford University Press, 125–146.

Pera-Ros, R., 2021. 'Ell, ella, elli'. In Junyent, C. (ed.), *Som dones, som lingüistes, som moltes i diem prou*. Vic: Eumo Editorial, 193–194.

Pérez, S. and Moragas, F., 2020. 'Lenguaje inclusivo: Malestares y resistencias en el discurso conservador'. In Kalinowski, S., Gasparri, J., Pérez, I. and Moragas, F. (eds.), *Apuntes sobre lenguaje no sexista e inclusivo*. Rosario: UNR Editora, 69–95.

Plataforma per la Llengua, 2019. 'The Catalan Language: 10 million European Voices'. https://bit.ly/3XAyuOc (accessed 15 April 2023).

Plummer, K., 2005. 'Critical humanism and queer theory'. In Denzin, N. K. and Lincoln, Y. S. (eds.), *The Sage Handbook of Qualitative Research*. Thousand Oaks: Sage, 357–373.

Popic, D. and Gorjanc, V., 2018. 'Challenges of adopting gender-inclusive language in Slovene'. *Studies in Language* 86, 329–350.

Pujolar, J., 2001. *Gender, Heteroglossia and Power: A Sociolinguistic Study of Youth Culture*. Berlin: Mouton de Gruyter.

Pujolar, J. and O'Rourke, B., 2022. 'Theorizing speakers and speakerness in applied linguistics'. *Journal of Applied Linguistics and Professional Practice* 16 (2), 207–231.

Romaine, S., 2006. 'Planning for the survival of linguistic diversity'. *Language Policy* 5, 441–473.

Rowlett, B. J. L., 2020. 'Second language socialization in the margins: Queering the paradigm'. *Multilingua* 39 (6), 631–662.

Ruiz Mantilla, J., 2020. 'Santiago Muñoz Machado: "Tenemos una lengua hermosa y precisa. ¿Por qué estropearla con el lenguaje inclusivo?"'. *El País Semanal*, 17 July 2020. https://elpais.com/elpais/2020/07/17/eps/1594981722_985896.html (accessed 15 April 2023).

Sallabank, J., 2022. 'Peer-to-peer endangered language transmission among adults'. In Hornsby, M. and McLeod, W. (eds), *Transmitting Minority Languages: Complementary Reversing Language Shift Strategies*. Cham: Springer, 191–216.

Santos, A. C. (ed.), 2023. *LGBTQ+ Intimacies in Southern Europe: Citizenship, Care and Choice*. London: Palgrave Macmillan.

Schmitz, J., 2021. 'Deaf-queer signing in process: A qualitative sociolinguistic study of "queering deafhood", "deafing queerhood", and "queer sign language style"'. *Sign Language Studies* 22 (1), 42–74.

Sczesny, S., Formanowicz, M. and Moser, F., 2016. 'Can gender-fair language reduce gender stereotyping and discrimination?' *Frontiers in Psychology* 7 (25), 1–11.

Shoham, A., and Lee, S. M., 2018. 'The causal impact of grammatical gender marking on gender wage inequality and country income inequality'. *Business and Society* 57 (6), 1216–1251.

Stonewall Cymru, 2016. *Geirfa* [Vocabulary]. www.stonewallcymru.org.uk/cy/cymorth-chyngor/geirfa (accessed 18 January 2023).

Surace, A., Kang, A., Kahler, C. W. and Operario, D., 2022. '"I'm gay with an asterisk": How intersecting identities influence LGBT strengths'. *Journal of Homosexuality*. First published online 8 December 2022. https://doi.org/10.1080/00918369.2022.2132579 (accessed 18 January 2023).

Tevanian, P. and Tissot, S., 2010. *Les mots sont importants*. Montreuil: Les éditions Libertalia.

Torres, L., 2018. 'Latinxs?' *Latina Studies* 16, 283–285.

Trenchs-Parera, M., Larrea Mendizabal, I. and Newman, M., 2014. 'La normalització del cosmopolitisme lingüístic entre els joves del segle XXI? Una exploració de les ideologies lingüístiques a Catalunya'. *Treballs de Sociolingüística Catalana* 24, 281–301.

Viennot, É. , 2018. *Le langage inclusif: Pourquoi, comment*. Donnemarie-Dontilly: Éditions iXe.

Vila, F. X., 2013. 'Catalonia'. In Extra, G. and Kutlay, Y. (eds.), 'Language rich Europe: Multilingualism for stable and prosperous societies'. *European Journal of Language Policy* 5 (1), 201–207.

Walpole, A., 2022. Interview with John Walsh, Dublin, 24 April.

Walsh, J., 2019. 'National identity and belonging among gay "new speakers" of Irish'. *Journal of Language and Sexuality* 8 (1), 53–81.

Walsh, J., 2022. *One Hundred Years of Irish Language Policy, 1922–2022*. Oxford: Peter Lang.

Welsh Government, 2017. *Cymraeg 2050: A Million Welsh Speakers*. https://bit.ly/4cgoONm (accessed 18 January 2023).

Welsh Government, 2023. *LGBTQ+ Action Plan for Wales*. www.gov.wales/lgbtq-action-plan-wales-contents (accessed 20 February 2023).

Woolard. K. A. , 2016. *Singular and Plural: Ideologies of Linguistic Authority in 21st Century Catalonia*. Oxford: Oxford University Press.

Woolard, K. A. and Frekko, S. E., 2013. 'Catalan in the twenty-first century: Romantic publics and cosmopolitan communities'. *International Journal of Bilingual Education and Bilingualism* 16 (2), 129–137.

Wright, L., 2020. *Critical Perspectives on Language and Kinship in Multilingual Families*. London: Bloomsbury.

Zimman, L., 2018. 'Transgender voices: Insights on identity, embodiment, and the gender of the voice'. *Language and Linguistics Compass* 12 (8): e12284.

Cambridge Elements ☰

Language, Gender and Sexuality

Helen Sauntson
York St John University

Helen Sauntson is Professor of English Language and Linguistics at York St John University, UK. Her research areas are language in education and language, gender and sexuality. She is co-editor of *The Palgrave Studies in Language, Gender and Sexuality* book series, and she sits on the editorial boards of the journals *Gender and Language* and the *Journal of Language and Sexuality*. Within her institution, Helen is Director of the Centre for Language and Social Justice Research.

Holly R. Cashman
University of New Hampshire

Holly R. Cashman is Professor of Spanish at University of New Hampshire (USA), core faculty in Women's and Gender Studies, and coordinator of Queer Studies. She is past president of the International Gender and Language Association (IGALA) and of the executive board of the Association of Language Departments (ALD) of the Modern Languages Association. Her research interests include queer(ing) multilingualism and language, gender, and sexuality.

About the Series
Cambridge Elements in Language, Gender and Sexuality highlights the role of language in understanding issues, identities and relationships in relation to multiple genders and sexualities. The series provides a comprehensive home for key topics in the field which readers can consult for up-to-date coverage and the latest developments.

Cambridge Elements $\equiv$

Language, Gender and Sexuality

Elements in the Series

A full series listing is available at: www.cambridge.org/ELGS